Caesar

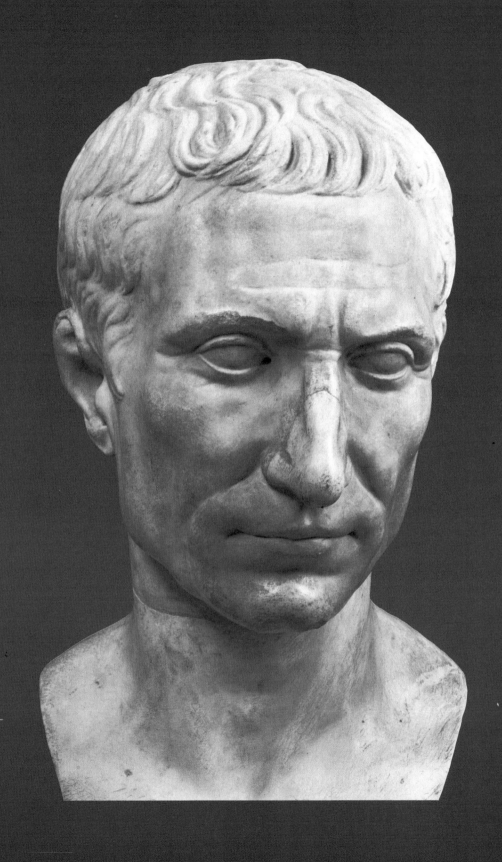

Caesar

Michael Grant

Introduction by Elizabeth Longford

Follett Publishing Company Chicago

First published in the
United States of America
1975 by
Follett Publishing Company,
Chicago

ISBN 0–695–80542–8
Library of Congress Catalog Card Number
74–21374

Printed in England

House editor Enid Gordon
Art editor Andrew Shoolbred
Layout by Florianne Henfield

Contents

Introduction

'I CAME, I SAW, I CONQUERED.' These are among the most out-rageous yet impressive words in the world. It is reassuring to know from Michael Grant's superb biography that Julius Caesar undoubtedly uttered them (though borrowing from the Greek) for they seem to sum him up. Not only did he conquer the ancient world, but his name re-echoed through the medieval and modern worlds also, and has never ceased to fascinate our own. Few can read his story without in some sense being conquered by the man's brilliant intelligence, unshakeable will and vast achievements, culminating in one of the most dramatic tragedies of all time – literally a crime club's masterpiece.

Michael Grant moves as freely and familiarly among the great classical figures – the Pompeys and Ptolemies, Antony and Augustus, Cicero, Catullus and Cato – as if he had known them personally. He shows that Caesar himself was not just the rather cardboard tyrant of Shakespeare's *Julius Caesar,* but a man of 'breeding, charm, heroic large-mindedness, humour'. Nor was Cleopatra the immature, kittenish seductress of Shaw's *Caesar and Cleopatra,* but a young woman of immense cleverness and ambition.

It is astonishing to realise how many projects or records set up by Caesar remained unfinished or unbroken until quite recently. His projected Corinth canal was completed only in 1893. The size of his Channel fleet sailing to conquer Britain in 54 BC was never again equalled until a British fleet sailed in the other direction in 1944 AD. It must have strengthened the already tough nerves of leaders like Wellington and Churchill, facing Napoleon and Hitler, to remember that Britain was one of Caesar's few failures. Nevertheless, our language, like so many others, gives prominence to many phrases from Caesar's extraordinary career.

Professor Grant tells us why we talk of 'crossing the Rubicon' and what meanings may be hidden in *'Et tu, Brute?'* To a British reader, the account of Caesar's epoch-making act by which he broadened the Senate sounds like a Roman version of the Great Reform Bill. But to the French we may be sure it evokes the political reforms of Napoleon. Caesar's bold attacks on problems

7

of currency, the calendar and the workless remind us that the age of the man-made computer has still something to learn from the age of the 'divine' dictator.

Caesar's dictatorship, however, is one of the things about him which are hardest to take. His greed for wealth, his womanising, violence and cruelty are others. These blots, especially the distinction he drew between Roman citizens and 'barbarians' as far as human rights were concerned, are all frankly faced and indeed underlined by Professor Grant. He points out that 'ruthless atrocities' were employed by Caesar to 'pacify' the barbarians, whereas his clemency towards Roman rebels became legendary.

Readers will welcome the delightful off-shoots of Professor Grant's scholarship; his care in giving modern as well as ancient place-names wherever possible; the lively and witty translations from Caesar and his famous contemporaries.

In the end, Caesar's eternal magnetism is seen to lie in two main directions. First, the unique spread of his genius over military, administrative and literary spheres. Second, the problem of his radicalism. Caesar was a radical pitted against conservatives. Every generation must ask itself whether radicalism, based on populist sympathies, can ever draw back from the abyss of dictatorship. An answer may be found by studying the crises and dilemmas of Julius Caesar's life.

Elizabeth Longford

Preface

THERE ARE MANY REASONS why the life of Julius Caesar deserves continual and continuing study. But perhaps the main reason is that he lived at the turning point between two great historical epochs – and stamped this vital moment of transformation with an imprint entirely his own. There are, of course, in reality no such things as separate epochs, because one merges directly into the next, without a definite point of transition between the first and the second. Yet if ever the distinction between two epochs by convenient labels of this kind may be regarded as justified, it was now, when the Roman Republic was gradually ending and the Roman Empire was gradually about to begin. Caesar came precisely at this juncture. Whether he should be regarded as the terminator of the old epoch or the inaugurator of the new has been endlessly debated, as each new generation of statesmen and students add their own particular contemporary preoccupations to the argument.

Such discussions rage with particular vigour because, of all the conspicuous figures of world history, Caesar was the most versatile, the most outstandingly able over the widest possible range. General, administrator, orator, man of letters, fascinator of women – he was good at all these activities, and not just good but outstandingly, exceptionally good at every one of them. No wonder so many legends have arisen about him. And it is our business to note these legends as part of the Caesar myth that has inspired, in one form or another, every successive age from his time up to Shakespeare's, and then on to our own; though it is our business, too, to discount the purely fictional elements as far as we can when we are endeavouring to reconstruct the facts of his life.

Perhaps what emerges most clearly from any such study is that, although Caesar surpassed almost everybody at almost everything, what he did best of all was to command troops in battle. It is therefore of peculiar interest to any British student to remember that one of his few failures was his inability to conquer England, an inability he shared with Napoleon and Hitler. When other enterprises of Caesar failed to come to fruition, as occasionally happened, it is usually possible to say that Caesar did the groundwork, and others

11

benefited from it at a later date. In the case of his two expeditions across the Channel, however, it is hardly permissible to claim this, because when southern England finally came to be conquered a century later, almost all the groundwork had to be done over again. So the English can boast that they alone defeated Caesar. And the French, on the other hand, unless they are too devoted to their Celtic heritage to offer such an assertion, can boast that, by suffering defeat at his hands, they laid the foundations of the Latin culture of France. Yet it was not his aggressions against the Gauls, or against the Britons or Germans for that matter, which tested him to the uttermost: his greatest battles were those fought against his fellow Romans.

Caesar's political life, though full of melodramatic excitements, often leaves a pretty grubby impression of cynicism and violence; and this raises two important questions. The first is whether the men who rule, or aspire to rule, great nations and empires can ever manage to keep their hands entirely clean for very long. For these huge and varied communities must inevitably throw up crises of one sort or another at fairly frequent intervals, and it is arguable that such crises, and all the major problems that are associated with them, can only be dealt with by urgent, drastic and ruthless action: that is to say, they can perhaps only be dealt with by the application of moral standards that would be unacceptable in private life, whether to ancient Romans or to ourselves. What is the solution? Certainly Caesar and his contemporaries did not find one, and it is not at all clear that we have found one today.

Another is this: was Caesar, on balance, a good influence upon world history, or a bad one? It may sound an excessively simple and naive query, begging every sort of question relating to the meaning of words. And yet, for centuries, it has exercised the attention of thousands of very subtle minds. Perhaps it could be framed rather differently: would you rather be ruled by the dictator Caesar, or by the Roman noblemen whom he superseded? It is a somewhat delicately balanced point. To be ruled by Caesar meant submission to a thoroughgoing autocrat, who was quite capable of visiting the most ruthless punishment on anyone who got out of line – a line drawn by himself. To be ruled, on the other hand, by the noblemen of the late Republic meant subjection to the wills of a corrupt, self-seeking, arrogant caucus of noblemen, whose slogan 'liberty' referred exclusively to their own unrestricted freedom of action and speech, and no one else's. Neither of these two different kinds of domination could be described as in the least desirable for its victims, and to build up either Caesar or his political enemies as saintly heroes, or, after their downfall, saintly martyrs, is entirely misleading. On balance, perhaps most of us would have preferred living under Caesar, whose administrative measures at least showed some concern for the welfare of the ordinary Roman.

However, Caesar did not live long enough to give full expression to such aims. If he had done so, he might have proved a good deal more radical than his cautious successor, Augustus. But it was left for Augustus to set his own stamp upon the new era for which Caesar had prepared. Yet how utterly different were their personalities! Augustus was endowed with all the cold, meticulous patience needed to establish a new order throughout the entire Roman world. Caesar, however, as far as his sudden death makes it possible to discern, had lacked this particular sort of patience altogether; or at least, in spite of his long memory in political matters, he never found time to show it. On the other hand the gifts which he *did* possess were of a gigantic variety that has been vouchsafed to no other man; and they deserve unending analysis and reassessment.

This book then is one more endeavour (not my first, though any reader patient enough to read both volumes will find different emphases and points of view) to sum up what Caesar did and what he thought. And I shall also hope to show what other people have thought about him, both in his own lifetime and among subsequent generations.

I am very grateful to Mrs Enid Gordon, of Messrs Weidenfeld and Nicolson Ltd, for all her editorial assistance.

Michael Grant *Gattaiola, 1974*

1 The Undermining

of the Republic

WHEN JULIUS CAESAR WAS BORN, in 100 BC, he was born into a Roman empire which had expanded and exploded far beyond its earlier narrow frame, so that everything had changed and was still rapidly changing.

For the first centuries of its existence, now many hundred years back, Rome had been a tiny state struggling for survival among other Italian tribes and peoples. Then, in the fourth century BC, it had established its supremacy throughout all the central regions of the peninsula. South Italy and Sicily had still lain outside the Roman sphere for a time, since they were virtually extensions of Greece, full of Greek-city states and known as 'Magna Graecia' in consequence. Soon after 300 BC, however, the Romans' increasing dealings with this Magna Graecia brought them into contact with Carthage, the north African maritime power of Semitic and near-eastern origin, which controlled the greater part of the western Mediterranean. In two massive Punic Wars, Rome conquered the Carthaginians, and then in the second century BC it was drawn into the eastern Mediterranean region as well, where it proceeded to overcome, one after another, the Greek kingdoms which had shared the heritage of Alexander the Great. At the time of Julius Caesar's birth, the Romans possessed provinces along huge stretches of the coast of what they called 'Our Sea', the Mediterranean, together with its hinterland (map 5).

Ever since the legendary expulsion of the kings in the remote past, Rome had remained a Republic. In form, it was a democracy, since the sovereign executive and legislative body was the Assembly, of which every Roman citizen was a member. In practice, however, the senate, although its functions were, officially speaking, not executive but advisory, was the traditional centre and source of power. From its three hundred members were elected, each year, the officers of state. The chief of them were the two consuls, and next in importance came the six praetors. After their year of office, consuls and praetors alike were entitled to receive a lucrative provincial governorship and command. In an emergency, a dictator could be chosen, and he took precedence over all these officials. But the tenure of dictators was limited to six months, and from the later third century BC onwards no appointments to this office were made for a hundred and twenty years.

The transformation of the little Roman city state into a great imperial nation had brought with it many other transformations too, economic, social and cultural alike. These changes had brought

PREVIOUS PAGES The Roman Forum from S.Francesca Romana.

16

ALPS

CISALPINE GAUL   Mantua

R. Po   Placentia

Mutina

Pistoria

Lucca

R. Rubicon

Ariminum

Arretium

R. Tiber

ADRIATIC SEA

Corfinium

Rome

Pomptine
(Pontine) Marshes — Tarracina (Anxur)

Formiae   Capua

CAMPANIA

Brundusium

Tarentum

SARDINIA

Italy

SICILY

Scale 0   50   100 miles

vast wealth, and had conferred vast potential authority upon the commanders of the large armies that the Republic now needed. There had likewise been changes in the internal political scene. Hitherto this had been a stage on which a few very powerful families, or their individual members, had engaged in constant cutthroat competition against one another, striving for office and its prizes, and mobilising whatever sections of the community they could to vote for them and lend them their support. But finally two opposed tendencies could be discerned within these intrigues – tendencies not sufficiently clear-cut to warrant the identification of opposed political parties, but well enough defined, all the same, to be differentiated by labels: the holders of the two different views were described as *optimates* and *populares*. The *optimates*, meaning the best people, were conservatives, who believed that the state was best guided by the senate, and that the people, that is to say the Assembly, ought to take whatever advice the senate gave it. The *populares*, on the other hand, were the people's men who tended to favour certain radical objectives such as long overdue land and judicial reforms; and they attracted the support of many of the knights who were the next most important order to the senators, and included men to whom the emergence of the empire had brought influence and wealth. The politicians who were known as *populares* were by no means proletarians, but were noble members of the senate just like their opponents. Yet in order to get their way, they saw no objection at all, whenever necessary, to appealing over the heads of the recalcitrant senate to the Assembly of the people, so that the senate's traditional conservative management of Roman affairs was set at risk.

Two young nobles of reformist tendencies, the brothers Tiberius and Gaius Gracchus, acted in this fashion with considerable determination, and met their deaths in riots (133, 122 BC). Later, in the year of Caesar's birth, the same fate befell a considerably more radical nobleman, Lucius Appuleius Saturninus. He had believed that he had Gaius Marius on his side: and Marius was the greatest general of his day. However, at the last moment Marius recoiled from the violent methods of Saturninus, and abandoned him.

Nevertheless, violence was destined to be the keynote of the century that was now starting – and the keynote of the life of Julius Caesar that started with it. While he was still a boy, Italy was convulsed by the Social War, in which many of the towns and communities of the peninsula (*socii*, allies) rebelled against their

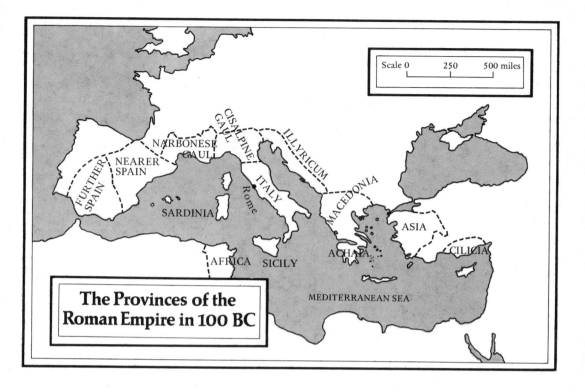

The Provinces of the Roman Empire in 100 BC

continued exclusion, insisted upon by the reactionary senate, from the vote and other privileges of Roman citizens (91–87 BC). Next followed bloodthirsty civil strife between the *populares*, led by Marius and then after his death by Cinna, and the *optimates* who rallied round the patrician Sulla. After Sulla's army had decisively prevailed, he did not immediately restore the traditional Republic, but instead assumed the ancient emergency office of dictator (81 BC), and assumed it not for the traditional maximum of six months, but for an indefinite period – which constituted a major step towards autocracy. Nevertheless, in the next year he was already beginning to revive constitutional senatorial government. For the whole purpose of his dictatorship had been to try to bolster up the power of the senate once again, by a series of measures in the conservative interest.

Caesar's family were both 'patrician' and 'noble' – the former term referring to the ancient inner circle of the highest aristocracy, which was not necessarily located in the centre of the political power structure, while 'nobility' was the term reserved for those families who belonged to the *political* inner circle, because they could boast   ancestors who had held the consulship. In recent

19

Roman Senators Going to the Forum, by Jean Lemaire (1598–1659)

21

times, the Julii, like other such patrician houses, had dropped out
of the struggle for power, because they lacked the great wealth
which was indispensable for its effective prosecution. However,
they had not stopped trying. Before the victory of Sulla, their
hopes had been especially based upon the *populares*, since Caesar's
aunt Julia was the wife of Marius, and Caesar himself married
Cornelia, the daughter of Marius' successor Cinna (84 BC). But when
Cinna was murdered, and two years later Sulla became the autocratic ruler of Rome, these connexions proved highly embarrassing.
Sulla's price for sponsoring Caesar's career was that he should
divorce Cinna's daughter and marry a woman of a family that
supported his own cause. But Caesar loved his wife – or perhaps he
was already looking beyond Sulla. In any case, he refused the
dictator's offer, and in consequence found himself deprived not
only of Cornelia's dowry but of an honorific post – a priesthood –
to which he had been appointed. An interview with Sulla went
badly. Caesar was a good-looking youth, tall, fair, slender, with a
rather full face, and keen black eyes. But Sulla disapproved of his
unorthodox clothes, since the young man wore a loose belt, which
was regarded as eccentric, and affected fringed sleeves reaching
down to his wrists. Moreover, he paid rather too careful attention
to the details of his personal appearance. For example, he was
accustomed to having superfluous hair removed with pincers. And
his hair was very meticulously arranged. Indeed, he was sometimes
seen adjusting his parting with one finger.

Since he had annoyed the ferocious dictator it seemed best to his
family to spirit him far away from the Roman scene. So they secured
him a post in north-western Asia Minor. There he enjoyed the
favour of Nicomedes IV, the king of Bithynia – an ostensibly
independent kingdom that was really a 'client' of Rome – and for
the rest of Caesar's life his enemies maintained that their relationship was homosexual. Probably they were right. Nevertheless
Caesar won a distinguished military decoration for some unknown
action off the west coast of the peninsula, and then proceeded to
its south-eastern region where he served on the staff of the governor
of Cilicia, who was concluding operations against pirates.

But soon after he arrived there, the news reached him that Sulla
was dead, and he decided to return to Rome without delay. Once
there, he embarked on the oratorical activity of a barrister. This
was a customary occupation for young upper-class Romans, since
almost their entire education consisted of training in oratory – and
indeed this was something on which the whole of Roman public

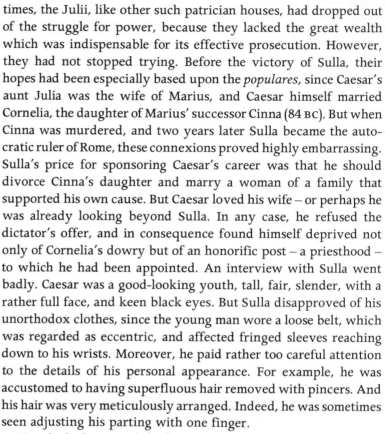

22

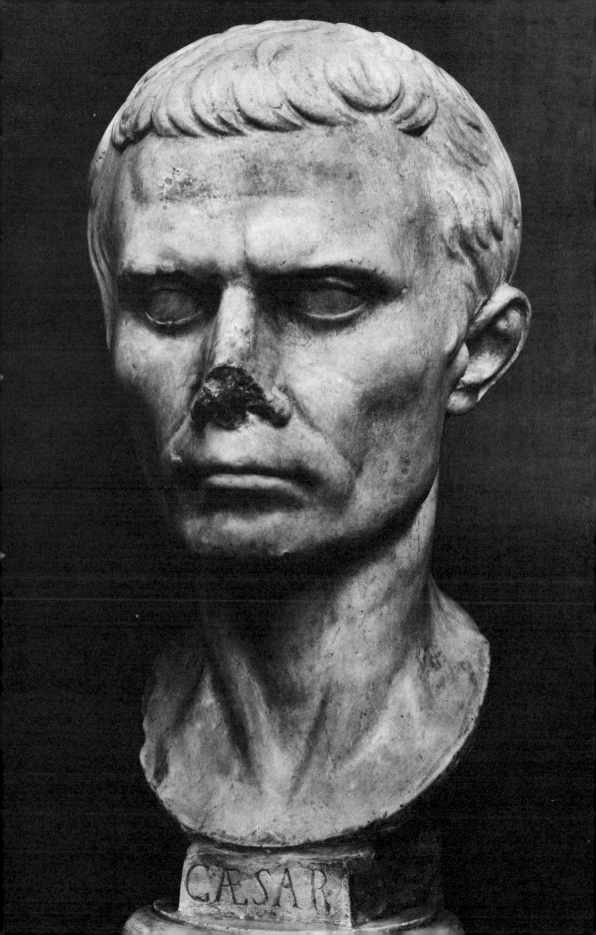

life depended. Now Caesar was a public speaker of the very highest order, and with the sole exception of Cicero, who was perhaps the greatest orator the world has ever seen, there was no one among his contemporaries who excelled him. 'Caesar is said', remarked the biographer Suetonius, 'to have delivered his speeches in a high pitched voice, with impassioned action and gestures, which were not without grace.'

The way in which an aspiring political orator could best make a name was by prosecuting provincial governors, whose bad financial record often made them singularly vulnerable to this form of attack. And that was what Caesar now set himself to do. In 77 BC he launched two charges of this kind. They were successful up to a point, because they made him friends among the people the two governors he was attacking had oppressed. But in neither case did he succeed in securing a conviction. In consequence, he decided that the study he had already devoted to public speaking, though well up to the usual standard of higher education achieved by a cultivated upper-class Roman, was not yet enough, and he went off to Rhodes to work under an eminent Greek rhetorician, Apollonius Molon. On the way to the island, however, Caesar was kidnapped by pirates. He raised the required ransom and was released, but soon afterwards he went after them with a body of troops and captured them: whereupon he took a drastic revenge by having them crucified.

Then he returned to the capital, and secured election to a priesthood, which, at Rome, was an amateur, part-time institution and did not therefore encroach on his career, while at the same time advancing him a good step up the ladder of political prestige. Next, he had a short preliminary spell of regular military service as a junior officer.

Within less than a decade after Sulla's death, the dictator's arrangements for bolstering up the authority of the 'best people' were beginning to be eroded. In consequence, it now seemed to Caesar, with his Marian marriage connexions, that the revival of the radical Marian cause of the *populares* might be the making of his own career. And so, in the very first speech he ever delivered before the Assembly (70 BC), he spoke in favour of granting an amnesty to Sulla's enemies who were still living in exile – including the brother of his own wife. Then, in the next year, his aunt Julia died; and the young Caesar was chosen to deliver her funeral speech. He employed the occasion to offer a double affront to the conserva-

tives. In the first place, he reminded them that the dead woman's genealogy and his own claimed a distinction which very few of them could claim, going back to the antique kings of Rome and to the goddess Venus herself.

But at the same time Caesar, while thus specifically claiming to outbid even the most aristocratic among the conservatives with his pedigree, also made it abundantly clear that he did not regard

An unknown Roman; perhaps a Chief Priest.

himself as one of their political persuasion. For his aunt, whose obituary speech he was delivering, had been the widow of Marius himself, the father figure of the *populares*. And so, in her funeral procession, Caesar boldly displayed statues or pictures of Marius. Now these had never once been on view since the dictatorship of Sulla, who had condemned the memory of Marius and had declared his friends public enemies and outlaws. That is to say, Caesar was deliberately flouting Sulla's policy, and challenging his heirs and supporters who were still in power, and indicating that he himself stood with their opponents who were still, at this stage, disorganised and demoralised. Shortly afterwards he repeated the gesture. For now his own wife Cornelia, who had borne him his daughter Julia, died. The funerals of young women were not usually accompanied by orations, but Caesar delivered a speech in her honour. Her father had been Cinna, the close associate and successor of Marius, and Caesar exploited the occasion by referring to him in eulogistic terms.

In spite of these attacks on the establishment, he now received a routine junior appointment, a quaestorship, for one year. However the job he was given was not one of the more influential quaestorships in the capital, but a post in Further Spain. There his duties were administrative and judicial. Yet when he talked to Romans and Spaniards in the province he could not fail to hear a great deal about a gallant soldier, Sertorius, who until only a short time previously had held Spain over a number of years for the Marian cause, against the government of the capital. But for Caesar Spain was only an interlude: his one desire was to return to Rome – the centre of the world – and he started back homewards at the earliest permissible moment, if not before. In the course of the journey, he arranged to stop for a time in a region that was of the utmost political and military importance. This was Cisalpine Gaul – now north Italy, between the Alps and Apennines, but at that time not part of Italy, and (north of the Po) not in possession of the Roman citizen rights to which all Italians were now entitled. An immensely abundant reservoir of human and natural resources, Cisalpine Gaul was indignantly conscious of its lack of the full franchise, and Caesar utilised the opportunity to do good turns to many people in the area, and to raise hopes that he might be able to get their status improved. Indeed, he stirred up trouble so effectively that the government, in its anxiety, now countermanded the marching orders of troops it had intended to dispatch to the east, keeping them close at hand instead.

Then, on his return to Rome, Caesar married again. His new wife was Pompeia, who was the granddaughter of Sulla. To marry a woman with this background seemed contrary to Caesar's Marian policy. But a factor that more than compensated for her Sullan antecedents was her wealth, which was extensive. At this stage in his career, and for many years still to come, financial considerations were of overriding importance to Caesar. To conduct a successful political career at Rome, as he fully intended to, very substantial resources were essential, and Caesar and his family, for all their glamorous patrician origins, just did not possess them. His marriage to Pompeia was an early step in the right direction. But it was a single step only; and in the years that immediately followed his position still remained wholly insignificant in comparison with the roles of two other men who had become, in their very different ways, national leaders – Crassus and Pompey.

Crassus was enormously wealthy: he was heard remarking that nobody could be described as a political force unless he could maintain an army on his own income – which would have caused him no difficulty. As for Pompey, as long ago as the 80s BC, when he was not yet twenty-five years of age, he had already greatly distinguished himself fighting for Sulla against the Marians; and after that he had succeeded in overthrowing the Marian leader Sertorius in Spain. Later, when Rome was confronted by a dangerous slave-revolt led by Spartacus, and finally, with great difficulty, brought it to an end, both Crassus and Pompey had claimed the credit for themselves. That was in 71 BC, and in the following year the two men had become consuls together. Pompey now proceeded to demonstrate that, although he had made his name under Sulla, he was not prepared to fall in with the conservative, aristocratic traditions the dictator had sponsored.

And soon afterwards, in 66 BC, a great new opportunity to establish himself as a national leader came his way. The Mediterranean coastlands were at this time gravely disturbed by pirates: and they received open encouragement from Rome's arch-enemy Mithridates VI, who, after two decades of hostility, still retained the kingship of Pontus in northern Asia Minor. The pirates had shown what they could do by kidnapping the young Caesar; and they were paralysing the communications of a large part of the empire. In 66 BC it was proposed by a tribune of the people, Aulus Gabinius, that the command against them should be entrusted to Pompey, so that he could destroy them once and for all. Most senators were horrified by the idea, which would, they felt, place

Late Republican architecture – the so-called Temple of Fortuna Virilis beside the Tiber in Rome.

a perilously large amount of power in his hands. However, Caesar enthusiastically supported the project. For not only was it desirable in itself, but he estimated that in order to make progress in Roman politics he was going to need Pompey's support.

Pompey secured his command, and destroyed the pirates in a brilliant campaign that only lasted three months. Then he was proposed for an even more significant commission, against the hitherto unconquerable Mithridates. Once again the conservatives adamantly opposed the suggestion, since it was an insult to their own protégé Lucullus, who had been holding this command. On the other hand Pompey's appointment was supported by the rising young orator Cicero. Although Cicero's political position was unpromising, since the absence of any consul from his ancestry meant that he was not 'noble' and he was not a wealthy

Bust of an unidentifiable Roman, perhaps a contemporary of Caesar's.

man either, he had made a name for himself four years earlier by attacking a conservative, Verres, for a widespread variety of malpractices committed as governor of Sicily.

It is also very likely that Caesar backed the proposal to give Pompey the appointment against Mithridates – just as he had backed his command against the pirates. For Caesar knew very well that before long he was going to need Pompey's support in his turn. Besides, he would find it convenient if Pompey remained far away from the Roman scene for a time. This was because the relations between Pompey and Crassus were now chilly, but Caesar needed to be on good terms with both of them – with Pompey because he was so prominent, and with Crassus because he was so rich. In consequence, the mutual unfriendliness between his two potential patrons caused him embarrassment; and it would

clearly be easier if he did not have to deal with both of them in the capital at one and the same time.

At the moment, he was glad to be able to concentrate on Crassus. For Caesar was extremely extravagant, partly in order to make political investments and partly just because he had luxurious personal tastes. As a result, he found himself heavily dependent upon Crassus. Moreover Crassus, happy to have an efficient and dependent henchman, was willing to respond. With his help, Caesar was appointed curule aedile in 65 BC. This office was primarily concerned with the maintenance of public buildings and order, and sounded rather dull. But it also provided rising politicians with a splendid opportunity to become popular by organising lavish entertainments for the populace. For example, these shows often included gladiatorial games and wild beast hunts. Caesar outdid all his predecessors in the spectacular nature of such displays; but he also specifically directed them towards political purposes by displaying statues of Marius and inscriptions celebrating victories he had won over German invaders.

The leader of the conservatives in the senate, Catulus, had long been suspicious of Crassus and Pompey, and now he deplored these activities of Caesar as well, which he interpreted as intrigues directed towards the seizure of political power, openly subversive of the traditional Republican system which Sulla had tried to revive. It is doubtful, however, whether at this stage Caesar intended any such far-reaching subversion, since what he had in mind above all else was the promotion of his own career. Meanwhile Crassus and Caesar remained busy on a variety of projects. In particular, they supported an important land-bill brought forward by a tribune of the people, Rullus, who proposed that public land in Rome and the provinces should be redistributed, and that a special commission should be appointed for the purpose. However, Cicero opposed Rullus' bill, and in spite of the advocacy of Crassus and Caesar it was defeated. But Caesar no doubt took this philosophically: the scheme had made a big splash, and it had won him friends who would be useful later on.

He was now thirty-seven, and at last his career took a decisive upward turn. For the office of chief priest (*pontifex maximus*) of the Roman state had become vacant, and to the general surprise he was elected to become the new incumbent. Reserved for the aristocracy and tenable for life, the chief priesthood, while in no way debarring its occupant from simultaneously holding other, secular posts, was a great political honour and weapon of patronage. Caesar's

OPPOSITE An Egyptian head of a priest, very probably to be identified with Julius Caesar.

OVERLEAF The remains of a fine building of Caesar's lifetime: the Basilica at Pompeii.

victory in the election was sensational, because he defeated two greatly senior competitors, including his critic Catulus. Caesar could play the card of his mythically grandiose origins against his rivals. But, above all, it was by cash supplied by Crassus that he outbid them – and, what is more, he knew exactly how much he needed to bid, because Catulus had attempted to secure the withdrawal of Caesar's candidature by bribery, thus unwisely revealing how much money he himself could afford to put down. On leaving home for the election Caesar had told his mother that, if he lost, he would not be coming back: since his debts would then force him to leave the country. But he won, and thus obtained a power-base from which he could eventually restore and extend his financial position. Moreover, as chief priest, he moved into the official residence attached to that post, the Regia adjoining the House of Vestals and the Forum.

Caesar was no believer in religion. But he was deeply attached to the national antiquarian traditions; and he also knew very well how to exploit them for political ends. Indeed, his interest in archaic practices and institutions appeared once again almost immediately, when he resuscitated an antique legal procedure that almost every-one else had forgotten. This was Trial for High Treason. Caesar revived this solemn procedure in order to prosecute an aged senator, Gaius Rabirius. Surprisingly enough, however, it was not with any recent offence that Rabirius was charged: what he was accused of was the murder of the well-known radical politician, Saturninus, no less than thirty-seven years earlier. However, Caesar's action was prompted by more topical motives than might appear. For Saturninus had been killed by men operating under one of the emergency decrees of the senate which had become a feature of the Roman scene during the second century BC. The formula adopted in these sweeping decrees was vague: *Let the consuls take measures that the state receive no harm.* But it was precisely this vagueness that Caesar and his radical fellow-*populares* feared, believing that, one day in the near future, it might lead to the senate assuming high-handed autocratic powers. Caesar himself, and his more moderate friends, were not necessarily against these decrees as such, but wished for safeguards against their abuse, and particularly against their employment to cause the deaths of Roman citizens. Rabirius was defended by Cicero and his trial petered out. But Caesar had made his point.

In the same year, the state was plunged into a major crisis. This was the Catilinarian conspiracy. An impoverished patrician of great charm but with a shady record, Catiline (Lucius Sergius Catilina) exercised considerable appeal among the many people plunged into ruin and destitution by the wars of the foregoing decades, and had sympathetic words for their grievances. By 64 BC, if not earlier, Crassus and Caesar had come to see him as a pliable potential satellite of their own. In consequence, when he was charged with atrocities perpetrated against the Marians as Sulla's subordinate, a special court, of which Caesar had been appointed president, proceeded to acquit him. True, Catiline's acts at that era had apparently been so brutal that Caesar, with his Marian sympathies, ought to have deplored them. But they had taken place a long time ago, and to protect a promising political ally they could be excused.

Soon afterwards, in July, 63 BC, came the elections for the state offices of the following year. Caesar was duly elected to a praetorship, second only to the consulship in the official hierarchy, and important because, like that office, it was normally followed by a provincial governor's post. Catiline was standing for a consulship of 63: having been prevented from offering his candidature on two previous occasions, he had at last succeeded in securing its recognition. But he was defeated. Right up to the time of this defeat it was probable that Caesar and Crassus had remained his political backers. Now, however, they dropped him utterly, without delay. For once he had failed at the polls – and it did not look as if he would be less unsuccessful in the future – he was of little use to them any more. Besides, it was rumoured that he was plotting violent revolution, and, whatever the more impecunious and impatient Caesar may have felt about it at the present stage, this was something to which the capitalist Crassus was wholly averse. The consuls appointed, when Catiline was rejected, were the worthless Gaius Antonius Hybrida (father of Mark Antony) and Cicero. For although Cicero was not a nobleman, the conservatives had finally decided to rally round his candidature, owing to their fears of the violent measures that Catiline might be planning.

What he was planning, in fact, as rumour rightly surmised, was to overthrow the state by force, with the help of desperate and displaced persons of all classes. As the new year began, and clearer knowledge of what he had in mind began to reach their ears, Crassus and Caesar, eager to exculpate themselves from damaging gossip, denounced their old accomplice to the consul Cicero – whose own private intelligence, meanwhile, was providing him with similar information. Cicero's subsequent magnificent

37

The House of the Vestal Virgins, with, in the background, the columns of the Temple of Castor and Pollux and the Tabularium.

39

The Temple of Saturn.

Catilinarian Orations, attacking Catiline and praising his own part in his detection and suppression have come down to us (in the literary form in which they were subsequently published), and from these we learn what happened next. The senate was induced to pass an emergency decree ordering that the plotters be struck down. Thereupon Catiline fled secretly from Rome and hastened into Etruria to mobilise his followers for a march on the capital. Meanwhile, close by the city itself, incriminating letters were seized from a visiting Gaulish delegation, and on the basis of these, five conspirators of high rank, including senators, were seized and placed under arrest.

Then, on 5 December, the senate was convened to consider the fate of the prisoners; and it proved to be one of the most famous meetings of all time. According to regulations, the first opinion had to be expressed by one of the members who had been elected to the consulship for the following year: and so it was a certain Decimus Junius Silanus who spoke. Silanus proposed that the men in custody, and four others who had not yet been arrested, should suffer the extreme penalty. The fourteen former consuls who were present did not demur. Then Caesar addressed the senate. It was a highly embarrassing moment in his career. To defend men unmistakably guilty of open rebellion was impossible. If, on the

41

other hand, he supported their execution, he would be retracting, not only his former personal association with Catiline, but his own declarations, earlier in the very same year, against the employment of emergency senatorial decrees to procure the deaths of Roman citizens. Nor could he very well remain silent; for, if he did so, his silence might well be counted against him by either or both sides later on.

The speech he delivered, in an effort to deal with this dilemma, seems to be faithfully reported by the historian Sallust. According to this account Caesar, while duly deploring the conduct of the conspirators, also argued that they should not be put to death, 'but that their goods be confiscated and that they be imprisoned in such towns as are best provided to undertake their custody'. It is not quite clear from this whether Caesar was proposing that the detainees should be imprisoned for life, or whether he envisaged that they should only be detained for the time being until the immediate crisis was past. In all probability, his immediate listeners were meant to suppose that he was advocating the former, severer, course, although he himself may also have had the other possibility in his mind, and may have intended later on, if need be, to say that this was what he had meant all the time.

His speech had a devastating effect on Silanus, who at once protested that his earlier speech had been misunderstood. When he had advocated the 'extreme penalty', he explained, he had not meant execution at all. but imprisonment. That is to say, he now decided, with an eye to the future, that it was wiser to give Caesar's proposal his support. And many other senators came to precisely the same decision.

Then Cicero, who as one of the consuls of the year was chairman of the meeting, made an equally careful speech in his turn. While seemingly moderate, he hoped to persuade his fellow-senators to agree that the prisoners should be put to death – and, what is more, he wanted them to take collective responsibility for this decision, so that the whole of the subsequent blame would not fall on himself alone. On the other hand a tribune elect, the thirty-two-year-old Cato, spoke in a far more downright fashion, specifically and vigorously advocating the capital penalty. Cato's repeated opposition to Caesar on every question from this time onwards, over a period of nearly two decades, was remembered as one of the major historical phenomena of the age, and he himself seemed to many subsequent generations the true standard-bearer of the Republic in its last years. Like his great-grandfather Cato the

Censor, one of the most famous and influential statesmen of the second century BC, he was a personage of great inflexibility, in whom the sternness of antique Romans and high-mindedness of Stoic philosophers merged as one. The younger Cato was an indomitable defender of his own aristocratic caste, yet at the same time the scourge of its many weaknesses – and, incidentally, of money-grubbers of all kinds, whether senators or knights. He hated Caesar, and Caesar hated him, and even many years later, after Cato was dead, Caesar's hatred still did not cease.

And so now, at this senate meeting about the prisoners, Cato savagely assailed Caesar's balanced analysis, declaring that all that had prompted its apparent motivation was Caesar's own guilty complicity in the very plot which was under discussion. Instead, Cato urged that the men under arrest should immediately be killed. He had his way with the senate, and on its orders Cicero ordered the execution of the conspirators, which was duly carried out.

43

First, however, Caesar, too, had narrowly escaped meeting his death, because as he left the senate-house Cicero's personal body-guard was only with difficulty prevented from lynching him. All the same, among a wide and varied circle of people his moderation in this historic debate had done his reputation good. Meanwhile, the immediate aftermath was quickly concluded: soon after Caesar, in the following month (January 62 BC), assumed the praetorship to which he had been elected in July, Catiline was compelled to fight a pitched battle against the government forces at Pistoria (Pistoia), and met his death.

The same year also witnessed a curious scandal at Caesar's own official residence. The occasion was a ritual in honour of the Good Goddess (Bona Dea), at which only women were supposed to be present. At the ceremony of 62 BC, however, a leading figure of Roman society – a radical nobleman in his mid-thirties named Publius Clodius – was found lurking on the premises, disguised in female dress. Accepting, or pretending to accept, a rumour that Clodius' purpose in undertaking this masquerade had been to make love to his wife Pompeia, Caesar promptly divorced her – a step he had perhaps been preparing to take anyway, especially as she had not borne him a child. But then Caesar provided a surprise. For whereas Cicero led a vituperative attack on Clodius for sacrilege, the allegedly injured husband himself, in combination with Crassus, secured the exoneration of the accused man. For in this able but strange personage they saw just the potential accomplice in their anti-conservative plans that Catiline had at first seemed to be, though he had subsequently failed to live up to their expectations.

However, even these somewhat sensational events were a storm in a tea-cup compared to what was happening in the eastern regions of the empire: to which all eyes were now turned. During the past three years, and more, Pompey had won unprecedented victories in those lands. His successes had enriched Rome with vast wealth, and had added the magnificent new province of Syria to the empire; while, in the process, Pompey had also enriched him-self so very greatly that he was now even wealthier than Crassus. This enhanced his attractiveness as an ally in the eyes of Caesar who, as the conqueror arrived back in Italy with forty thousand devoted legionaries, took the lead in proposing massive honours for the victorious commander.

He had no intention of breaking with Pompey – or for that matter,

45

Recitation of the ritual of
Dionysius, on a Pompeian
wall-painting of the first
century BC.

with Crassus. But at this juncture he did not have to perform the balancing trick involved in remaining friends with them both, for in 61 he left to govern the province to which his praetorship of the previous year had entitled him. This was Further Spain, consisting of the southern part of the peninsula (Baetica), a Romanised and peaceful territory, and the western part (Lusitania), which was un-Romanised and turbulent. In Lusitania – that is to say in the mountains of Portugal and westernmost Spain – Caesar conducted minor military operations against tribesmen, and this warfare had two important effects on his future. One was psychological: he discovered, or confirmed, that he had a talent for generalship. The second effect was financial. He contrived, by methods that were not regarded as illegal, to make himself a good deal of money from plunder and presents – which was just what his political career needed. He also made profits not only for himself but for his soldiers, who hailed him as their victorious commander (*imperator*). And he did not forget to send part of the proceeds to the right people at Rome, who, instead of subjecting him to the charges of illicit gain which were so often incurred by predatory governors, voted him a Triumph.

Moreover, quite apart from his military activities, Caesar's tenure of the Spanish governorship had brought him another form of experience that would prove useful in subsequent years. After many wars, the province had become crippled by debt and ravaged by formidable debt laws – typical of the ancient world – which allowed creditors to take possession of the entire income of their debtors. Now Caesar enacted that the creditors could not take it all, but only two-thirds. In modern times that still seems very harsh, but in his day it was a substantial and even radical reform. It also earned him grateful supporters who, when the time came, would prove very useful.

However, like so many Romans when they went to the provinces, Caesar had only one desire, and that was to return to Rome. He was entitled, according to the law, to try to become consul in 59 BC; that is to say, to stand as a candidate in the elections of July 60. If, however, he wanted to avail himself of this right, there were legal technicalities which meant he would be obliged to forego his Triumph. These juridical obstacles could have been overcome, if the senate had exhibited the goodwill to do so, but Cato ensured that they should not: and that was the end of any hopes that conservatives and Republicans would receive cooperation from

Caesar for all time to come. Moreover, this was not the only way in which they snubbed this too ambitious politician. For, when the senators came to allocate the provincial commands that the consuls of 59 BC should be given at the end of their years of office, they proceeded to allocate them a minor forestry commission instead – true, it was not yet known officially who the consuls were going to be, for they had not yet been elected, but the affront was directed at Caesar whose election was probable. Meanwhile the senate had also snubbed Pompey very gravely indeed. For, unimpressed and indeed alarmed by his enormous victories, they went so far as to refuse to pass the land-law providing rewards for his troops. It must be admitted that Pompey, while engaged in his reorganisation of the east, had decided a great many things on his own authority without consulting the senate. All the same, it was clear that, by refusing to reward his legionaries, the senate had inflicted on him the worst humiliation suffered by any Roman general of the century.

So the middle months of 60 BC saw Pompey and Caesar both nursing grievances against the conservatives: and this common interest brought them together. In July, Caesar was duly elected as one of the next year's consuls – unfortunately for him, the other consulship went to a diehard who viewed him with great hostility, Marcus Calpurnius Bibulus. Shortly afterwards Pompey and Caesar came to a secret understanding. There remained the problem of Crassus, whose jealousy of Pompey's victories had united him with the opponents of the land-bill to provide for his troops. Since then, however, Crassus too had been humiliated by the senate. For Crassus was an especially strong supporter of the propertied class next to the senators, namely the knights, who conducted much of the financial business of the empire. And now he had sought an important, if unreasonable, financial concession on their behalf – comprising a rebate for the tax-farmers, dependents of the knightly order who, in recent transactions, had imprudently overestimated their probable profits. But the senate had ensured that the concession should be turned down. Cicero, although he knew their demand was unreasonable, had regretted its rejection all the same, since it meant, as he saw, that even the most fragile pretence at a harmony between the principal different interests in the state was at an end.

And so it proved. Caesar, though still much less influential than either Pompey or Crassus, took the initiative in bringing them together. Whereupon the three men formed an informal but powerful association with one another, known to us as the First Triumvirate. At first, the partnership remained secret. Cicero was invited to join this conspiracy, because his oratory, and the prestige he had gained as consul, would be useful. But he saw fit to refuse. One of the reasons why he took this decision was his jealousy of Pompey, whose eastern successes had wholly eclipsed his own Catilinarian triumph. Moreover, Cicero was perhaps the first man – as he himself afterwards claimed – to realise the grave danger to the ancient Republican system presented by the unscrupulousness of Caesar, whom he 'feared as one might fear the smiling surface of the sea'.

Besides, Cicero, for all his vacillations and vanities, was always resolutely opposed to autocracy. He was opposed to it both from an idealistic motive and for a reason that was practical and self-regarding. On grounds of deeply felt principle, he genuinely deplored any suppression of the free workings of Republican institutions. But another reason why he deplored such totalitarianism – like other leading Romans – was because it meant that henceforward the honours and spoils of power were destined to go to the autocrats instead of themselves.

In seeing this First Triumvirate as an autocracy, Cicero was perfectly correct. Through the decade that followed, its rule was superimposed upon the Republican system, as a supreme controlling force which its enemies could only defy at great peril. Informal though the compact was, it effectively paralysed the free operation of the state; and some historians, with a good deal of plausibility, saw the moment when the triumvirate was established as the decisive sign that the Republic itself was coming to an end. Nevertheless, Cicero's condemnatory attitude must not be accepted without a major reservation. It was not just a case of autocracy against democracy, of black against white. The 'free' Republic that was now being superseded was not a democracy, and never had been. It had long been governed by tough, unprogressive and dishonest cliques, whose incompetence to govern the large empire was now painfully clear. These cliques were now replaced by a board of three, who were exceptionally able men, and for the time being were united in their aims. In the end, they were destined to fail, because their unity could not be maintained. Yet their noble enemies would have failed as well – and for the same reason, because they would inevitably have become divided among themselves.

When Caesar, in company with his enemy Bibulus, assumed the

consulship at the beginning of 59 BC, Pompey relied upon him to give his veterans their delayed rewards, and he was not disappointed. For one of Caesar's first actions was to propose a land-bill which earmarked the remaining public lands of Italy for the settlement of these men. The rich territory of Campania, where such lands were particularly extensive, was for the time being omitted, but the remaining regions were to be settled under the direction of a special commission, which was also, according to an additional far-sighted provision, instructed to include drafts of impoverished city-dwellers among the colonists. When Caesar brought up this proposal, he behaved according to strict constitutional tradition: for, before submitting the proposal to the Assembly for approval as a law, he first invited the senators for their observations in the customary fashion. In the senate, however, Cato opposed the plan with great force, interpreting this distribution of land as red revolution. But when, in desperation, he tried to talk the bill out, Caesar (who often found Cato exceptionally irritating) placed him under arrest. Shortly afterwards, realising that this was too high-handed an action, he let the prisoner go again. But meanwhile the senate had lost its opportunity to offer a constructive land policy, and the opportunity was never destined to recur.

Meeting with this negative attitude, Caesar decided to bypass the senate, and followed the custom of radical *populares*, referring his bill direct to the Assembly instead. There, to the general surprise, not only Pompey but Crassus, too, supported the measure, and so the full resources of the First Triumvirate were revealed. Amid scenes of open violence, in which Caesar's enemy Bibulus received rough handling, the bill became law, and the senate was cowed and coerced into submission. The irregularity of these and other proceedings conducted by him in the senate, and in the Assembly as well, was held against him for the rest of his life. A bitter joke went the rounds suggesting that Pompey was the king of Rome, and Caesar, in view of his alleged homosexual past, the queen – who now aspired, according to Bibulus, after the masculine, kingly role instead.

In fact, however, the links between the triumvirs were continually becoming stronger and stronger. Caesar secured a generous financial concession for Crassus' aggrieved knights, and ensured the ratification of Pompey's political and administrative arrangements in the east. Moreover, as well as embarking on a new marriage himself (his wife was Calpurnia, daughter of Piso, who

was destined for the next year's consulship), he also gave his only child, the seventeen-year-old Julia, to Pompey as his bride – and, although there was a difference of thirty years between them, the marriage proved an outstanding success. As things were now, the two men needed one another's services more than either of them needed Crassus; and henceforward, at meetings of the senate, it was noted that Caesar did not ask Crassus to speak until he had called upon Pompey first. Furthermore, once again in Pompey's interests, Caesar now took steps to enlarge his recent land-law so as to include Campania, the vital region that had been omitted from the previous bill. This was a tougher measure than the last one, since the compensation terms for the dispossessed owners of the land were far less generous than before – and once again there was violence. A law was also passed to curb the embezzlements of provincial governors, though, out of deference to Crassus, nothing was said about the knights who had so many financial interests abroad, and were equally predatory. Yet another bill sponsored by Caesar insisted that all future transactions of the Assembly and the Senate should be published for all to read. This measure was salutary and overdue; though its intention was mainly political, since it was designed to ensure that conservative obstruction to radical laws should not remain unknown to the public as a whole.

Caesar and Pompey also got their hands onto the wealth of the kingdom of Egypt. Even if it only maintained a shadow of its former proud independence, this realm of the Ptolemies, the successors of Alexander the Great, was still so enormously wealthy that the eyes of Roman politicians had been longingly turned towards it for a good many years. Crassus had shown a particular interest, but on the present occasion it was not so much he as his two colleagues who came to the aid of the distressed Egyptian king Ptolemy XII the Piper. As his support from his own Greco-Egyptian ruling class waned, his throne showed every sign of tottering: but Pompey and Caesar now agreed to induce the Roman senate to confirm his royal title and thus strengthen his position. However the price they exacted was enormous. It amounted to thirty-six million *denarii* – a sum which cannot be translated simply into terms of modern currency, but was so gigantic that even Ptolemy, with all his wealth, could only raise it by borrowing. So he called upon a Roman financial speculator, Gaius Rabirius Postumus (nephew of the man whom Caesar had recently prosecuted) for the required loan, and Caesar and Pompey got their money.

ABOVE King Ptolemy XII the Piper, of Egypt.

OPPOSITE The Tabularium, or record office, of Rome, built in 78 BC by Caesar's enemy, Catulus.

2
The First
Conquest of Gaul

So CAESAR, LIKE HIS TRIUMVIRAL COLLEAGUES, was now becoming a good deal richer. But the only way he could become even richer still, as he needed to be, was by securing a lucrative province when his consulship came to an end. It was precisely in order to scotch this ambition that the senate had voted the consuls of 59 BC the insultingly trivial province consisting of the forests and cattle-runs. Now this had to be changed, and to change it Caesar made use of an able, vulgar tribune, Publius Vatinius. Refraining, in the true radical fashion, from consulting the senate, Vatinius induced the Assembly to allot Caesar an incomparably better province than the cattle-runs – indeed, a double province, since the command that now came to him comprised both Cisalpine Gaul (North Italy, still not part of Italy itself) and Illyricum (coastal Yugoslavia). Moreover, his tenure was not to be limited to the customary one year or even two, but would last for no less than five years. Amid torrents of reciprocal abuse the law conferring this command was passed. To Caesar, this was not altogether unsatisfactory. For Cisalpine Gaul was rich and thickly populated, a great potential recruiting-ground – and Caesar, who had long fostered a close connexion with the region, at once proceeded to flatter its inhabitants as though they were Roman citizens, which for the most part they were not. The three legions now allocated to him he stationed at Aquileia, in the extreme north-east of Cisalpine Gaul. This was because it was in the other, closely adjoining area of his command, namely Illyricum, that the military operations which were intended to make his name as a commander were designed to take place. True, Illyricum, with its mountainous hinterland, was not an ideal theatre for spectacular campaigns. Yet although its coastline had long been, in somewhat desultory fashion, subjected to Roman control, this had never firmly extended inland, and that was what Caesar now proposed to accomplish. It was probably his intention to lead his army northwards as far as the River Save or Drave, or even, if all went well, as far as the Danube.

At this stage, however, an event occurred which changed his plan completely. This was the death of a Roman nobleman who had been allotted Rome's other Gallic province. This second province was Transalpine Gaul, or southern France, known also as the Narbonese province after its capital Narbo (Narbonne). Transalpine or Narbonese Gaul had been a Roman province for half a century, since the time when its annexation had been thought necessary to protect Rome's ally the Greek city state of

56

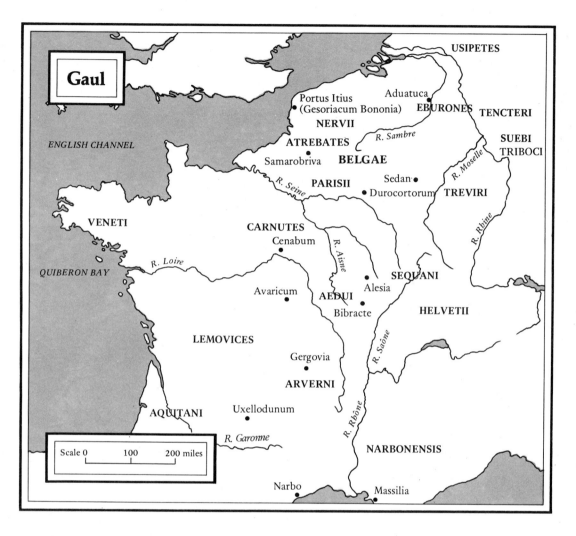

Massilia (Marseille) against the Gaulish tribes of the interior.

Since then, however, major upheavals among these tribes themselves had continued and intensified, until their constant strife with one another became a matter of serious concern to the Romans, who feared that it would overflow into their own province. Now, therefore, that the news of its governor designate's death became known, Caesar at once coveted the province for himself. For it was in Gaul rather than Illyricum, as he immediately decided, that the most remarkable opportunity of winning great victories presented itself. Not that he proposed to give up the province he had already voted. For success in Illyricum might well be obtainable later, and Cisalpine Gaul was still needed for the

57

recruitment of soldiers, so that both these regions must still be retained in his command. And all this he secured: the allocation of Narbonese Gaul, and the retention of Cisalpine Gaul and Illyricum as well. However, in order to disarm the senate's understandable suspicions of an excessive military authority – suspicions which were already being emphatically voiced by Cato – the tenure of the Narbonese province, unlike the other two, was initially to be for one year only, and then subject to renewal: though, in the event, this restriction proved meaningless.

When the time should eventually come for Caesar to leave Rome to take up his command some senators were going to heave a great sigh of relief. Others, perhaps, entertained even more radical plans for getting rid of him, and eliminating Pompey as well, since there were said to be plots against both their lives, and conservative leaders may have been behind plans of such a kind. When rumours of these conspiracies became known, Pompey, at least, became somewhat rattled. He was also more than a little embarrassed about the toughness of some of the methods that Caesar had been employing. Yet it had to be admitted that these methods produced results. For example, after disturbances had caused the consular elections for the following year to be repeatedly postponed, the triumvirs' candidates, Piso and Gabinius, were finally elected, and once again it was Caesar who achieved the desired result.

Nevertheless, the various acts of violence and other improprieties which he had committed during his tenure of the consulship meant that, from now onwards, he could only, according to Roman law, avoid utter ruin by remaining continually in public office: for if ever, even for a moment, he lost the immunity conferred by such an office, then prosecution for a variety of offences, including high treason, would immediately descend on him and his ruin would be assured. This future prospect became abundantly clear during the very first days after the conclusion of his consular year, when two of the new praetors proposed to the senate that all his acts and enactments as consul should be declared invalid and formally cancelled. In three speeches, which have regrettably not survived, Caesar dealt with his enemies' charges and endeavoured to rebut them. Then, however, without waiting for the senate's decision, he considered it advisable to move outside Rome, since once away from the capital he was already a governor exempted from prosecution. And so, not inside the walls of the city but in their immediate environment, he spent three months completing the preparations for his impending campaigns in Transalpine Gaul.

He also enlisted the services of a suitable man to represent him at Rome while he was away. This was Publius Clodius, whom he had protected four years earlier from conviction for sacrilege. Clodius was a talented radical freelance of marked eccentricity, who could be relied upon to instruct the numerous urban guerrillas at his disposal to lay about them with great ferocity. With this in mind the triumvirs duly secured Clodius' election as one of the tribunes of the people for the year 58 BC. Thereupon he at once secured great popularity among the people of Rome by passing a law which authorised the distribution of grain free of charge. Next he smartly arranged the ejection from Rome of the triumvirate's two most adamant enemies. First, Cicero, detested by Clodius whom he had tried to destroy, found himself arraigned for his leading part in the execution of the Catilinarian leaders more than four years earlier. Caesar was glad enough that Cicero should be removed from the Roman scene, but tried to clothe his removal with honour by offering him posts abroad. When Cicero, however, refused all these overtures, his conviction and banishment became inevitable: and without even waiting for Clodius' censure proposal to become law, he fled across the sea to Macedonia, to spend the most miserable sixteen months of his entire life. And then Cato, too, was removed from the scene. At Clodius' instigation, he received instructions to go to Cyprus to arrange for its annexation by Rome: and, somewhat surprisingly, he went. So Caesar could proceed to Gaul with the pleasant consciousness that two of the men who disliked him most had been removed from the political scene.

Ahead of him, though neither he nor anyone else knew it, lay eight years of fighting, mostly in the northern, western and central areas of France, the regions of Transalpine Gaul that lay beyond the Narbonese province and the existing boundaries of the empire. The nearer portions of this huge unconquered territory, lying between the Garonne and the Seine, were inhabited by two hundred independent tribes of Celtic Gaul, whereas the populations north of the Seine (the lands that are now north-eastern France and Belgium) comprised tribes of Belgae, people of German origin who had intermarried with the Celts. In the south-west of Gaul resided the Aquitani, who were not of Celtic race. The famous first words of Caesar's *Gallic War*, 'all Gaul is divided into three parts', refers to the Gauls (Celts), the Belgae and the Aquitani.

A coin of the Arverni.

In many parts of the country there was a high standard of prosperity, derived from agriculture, animal-breeding and metallurgical skills. But political cohesion between the Gallic tribes was almost non-existent, and within each individual tribe, too, chronic instability continually prevailed. In consequence, the capacity of the peoples of Gaul for serious warfare or self-defence was only limited. It is true that their cavalry, mounted by their ruling classes, was by no means negligible, and the trousered infantry, too, with their long cutting swords and wooden or wattle shields, could launch a terrifying initial charge. But once this had been steadfastly resisted the attacking mass soon degenerated into a disorderly rabble.

The most important tribes of central Celtic Gaul, round which Roman policy revolved, were the Arverni (Auvergne) based on their fortress-capital Gergovia, the Aedui centred on Bibracte (Mont Beuvray, above Autun) and the Sequani who lived along the Franco-Swiss border with their capital at Vesontio (Besançon). These tribes lay respectively north-west, north and north-east of the province of Narbonese Gaul: the Upper Loire was roughly the dividing line between the Arverni and the Aedui, and the Aedui and Sequani lived on either side of the Rhône. In course of time, the Arverni had been succeeded by the Aedui as the principal allies of the Romans. Like other major Gallic peoples, they were both surrounded by a ring of smaller dependent tribes, and the existence of these two nuclei, though it confirmed the impossibility of Gallic unity, at least created a certain fragile balance in the central part of the country. Now, however, the attention of the Romans had been drawn to a factor which gravely imperilled this balance. The peril came from the Helvetii, a Celtic people who had been driven out of their homeland in Germany and had settled in Switzerland. But there, too, they continued to be harassed by their German neighbours, and in 61 BC the Helvetic chiefs came to a fateful and far-reaching decision. For they determined to set their tribe moving once again, and to impel it in a westward direction. Travelling as an entire people, and carrying contingents of German allies in their wake, the Helvetii added up, Caesar learnt, to no less than 368,000 individuals, including 92,000 men fit for military service. Moreover, this vast horde had no intention of stopping until they had traversed the whole of Gaul, from its eastern to its western extremity, where they hoped to settle down and create new homes on the shores of the Atlantic.

The Romans came to the conclusion that this mass migration

must be stopped. It was certain, they argued, to encroach upon the northern frontier of their own Narbonese province. Or, even if it did not, the disturbances the great trek was bound to cause would pose an intolerable threat to the province's security. It was largely because of the development of this alleged menace that Caesar sought and secured the inclusion of Transalpine Gaul in his command. And then, as soon as possible after the termination of his consular year and the military preparations that immediately followed, he hastened northwards. By March 58 BC the massive and prolonged operations that we speak of as Caesar's Gallic War had begun.

A coin of the Arverni.

We know many details of Caesar's conquest of Gaul because he himself has given them to us in his *Gallic War* – a description far superior to any other account of warfare by a Roman, at least for another four centuries to come. The *Gallic War* and subsequent *Civil War* were entitled *Commentaries*, a term which, with unwarranted modesty, deliberately falls somewhat short of 'Histories', denoting rather a set of commander's dispatches or memoranda, amplified partly by speeches (intended, as always in antiquity, to give background rather than represent exact words) and partly by a somewhat sparing infusion of informative material of other kinds. Caesar's enormous brain-power and exceedingly lucid, compact, Latin style transform this apparently unambitious work into nothing less than a major masterpiece. The fact that the Roman commander-in-chief was its author (except for the last of its eight books, which was written by one of his generals, Aulus Hirtius) brings great advantages and disadvantages alike. The advantages lie in the extraordinary authority conferred by the author's unique inside knowledge, and by all the manifold talents which he could bring to bear upon its presentation to the reader. The disadvantages reside in Caesar's personal preoccupations, and most of all his desire to refute his political enemies in Rome. This sometimes induced him to magnify, minimise and distort – though it is usually the implications rather than the facts that suffer, since Caesar, apart from a certain exaggeration of impressive statistics, was far too good a hand at publicity to lie more than was absolutely necessary. Napoleon was only one of many great leaders who volunteered unstinting praise of the magnificent *Gallic War*. But it is a curious irony that European educational systems, because of Caesar's relatively easy Latin and 'leadership' qualities, have often made the work required reading by very young children, for whom the *Commentaries* can only be of limited value since the

61

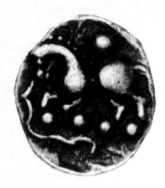

A coin of the Helvetii.

appeal of these writings, in substance and style alike, is a mature and sophisticated one.

Caesar's political preoccupations are especially apparent in his account of the first year's operations (58 BC) – which his opponents at Rome declared he ought never to have undertaken at all. The Helvetii, they asserted, were no concern of the Roman empire, since it was not part of their intention to encroach on the province. Caesar, on the other hand, was obliged to present them as a much more serious threat, in order to warrant his campaign against them. This he proceeded to launch at the earliest possible moment. Marching for eight days, and covering ninety miles a day, he and the bulk of his army of four legions were soon at Genava (Geneva). There he ordered the demolition of the bridge over the Rhône, and the blockage of all other possible routes that the Helvetii might try to follow towards the west. As a result, the tribe decided to move across Gaul by a more northerly route instead. This might have embarrassed Caesar, on the grounds that the threat to the Narbonese province had now diminished, so that it was no longer necessary for him to fight. But he refused to accept this conclusion, and instead reinforced his army, bringing two recently recruited legions from Cisalpine Gaul. Moreover, at this juncture, and no doubt at his own instigation, the pro-Roman government of the tribe of the Aedui appealed to him for military assistance against the Helvetian peril: so that a new excuse for Roman intervention was now available.

Thereupon Caesar attacked the migrating horde, and in a massacre on the River Saône a great number of them, perhaps a quarter of their total strength, were slain. After a vain attempt to parley with the Romans, the remainder got across the river, and pressed onwards. After pursuing them for two weeks, Caesar was held up by a failure in his grain-supply, which compelled him to make a seventeen mile detour to Bibracte (Mont Beuvray) to secure further provisions. The Helvetii, perhaps believing that he did not dare to attack them after all, began to harass his rear: and before long, at Armecy near the River Arroux, the clash came. This engagement, the first important battle of Caesar's career, is best described in his own words – though, as always, he creates an atmosphere of objectivity by naming himself in the third person.

Observing the action the enemy were taking, Caesar withdrew to a hill close at hand and sent out his cavalry to meet the enemy's attack. In the meantime he formed up his four veteran legions in three lines half-way up the hill, and posted the two recently levied in Italy on the summit with all the auxiliaries [non-Italian troops], so that the whole of the hillside above him was occupied with troops. The baggage and packs he ordered to be collected in one place, and defence works to be dug round them by the veterans posted in the top line. The Helvetii, who were following us with the whole of their transport, now parked it all together, and, after repulsing our cavalry with a battle-line drawn up in very close order, formed a phalanx and climbed towards our first line.

Caesar had all the horses – starting with his own – sent away out of sight, so that everyone might stand an equal danger and no one have any chance of flight. Then he addressed the men and joined battle. By throwing down spears from their commanding position the troops easily broke the enemy's phalanx, and then drew their swords and charged. The Helvetii were much hampered in action because a single spear often pierced more than one of their overlapping shields and pinned them together; and, as the iron bent, they could not pull them out. With their left arms thus encumbered it was impossible for them to fight properly,

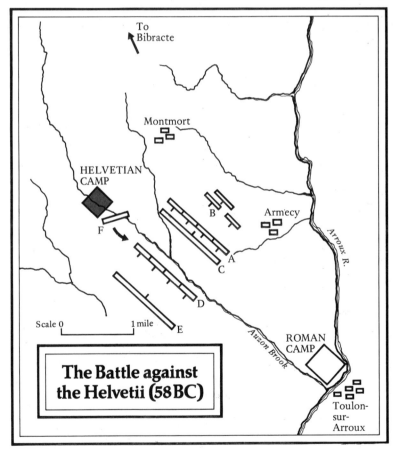

The Battle against the Helvetii (58 BC)

63

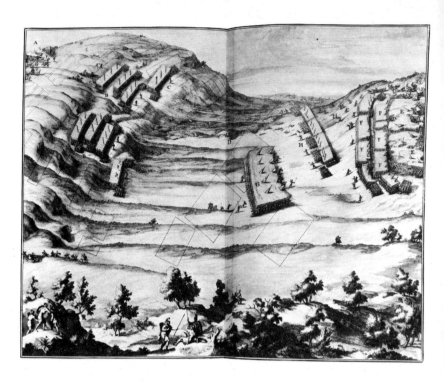

Reconstruction of Caesar's battle against the Helvetii (58 BC).

and many, after repeated attempts to jerk their arms free, preferred to drop the shields and fight unprotected.

At length, exhausted by wounds, they began to fall back towards a hill about a mile away.

(Caesar, *Gallic War*, I, 24–5)

It was the beginning of the end for Caesar's foes. Their German allies attempted a flank assault, which encouraged the Helvetii themselves to turn and attack again, but both forces were beaten off, and finally Caesar captured their camp. 130,000 of the Helvetii managed to disengage, and continued their westward journey, but their numbers gradually diminished, and before long the survivors were forced to turn back towards the homes they had vacated in Switzerland. In the course of all these events, Caesar boasted (no doubt exaggeratedly) that 258,000 Helvetii had met their deaths – including many old people and women and children.

Once the Helvetii were dealt with, he immediately turned to another and somewhat more authentic menace, which likewise came from the east. This time the threat came from the Germans. Rome had a terrifying recollection of these people who, fifty years earlier, had surged down as far as Italy itself, where the great Marius had finally destroyed their migrant tribes, the Cimbri and

64

A barbarian prisoner, on the
Triumphal arch at
Carpentras; perhaps of early
imperial date.

Teutones. Caesar, in his *Commentaries*, wants to stress that the current threat in 58 BC was equally grave; and in consequence he paints a careful contrast between the nomadic German hordes and the more settled peoples of Gaul who were confronted by these ferocious assailants from across the Rhine. This is a contrast which he derived from Greek scholarship of a generation or two earlier,

66

and bequeathed to future historians. But it was scarcely justified in his own time, since Celts and Germans alike resided on both sides of the Rhine, and no clear pattern of racial distribution or characteristics can have been perceptible.

Yet at the time when Caesar came to Gaul, its inhabitants were genuinely imperilled by one group of German tribes, known to the Romans as the Suebi, who had gradually been abandoning their nomad tendencies in favour of an increasing desire to seize fertile lands for permanent occupation. In the later 70s BC, Ariovistus, the chieftain of one of the Suebic peoples (perhaps the Triboci), was subjecting the Gauls who lay west of him to severe pressures. The Sequani, who were at this time engaged in a dispute with their neighbours the Aedui, imprudently invited him to attack these hostile compatriots of theirs, which Ariovistus did with success. More Germans then flocked into eastern Gaul, and in 61 BC Ariovistus and his allies inflicted a crushing defeat on the Aedui at a place named Magetobriga (possibly Moigte de Broie). Two years later, on the initiative of Caesar, Ariovistus had secured recognition as king and ally of the Roman people. But now Caesar himself, having arrived in Gaul, reversed this attitude, for he saw the prospect of another and even more dramatic campaign. To elicit Gaulish requests for help against Ariovistus was easy enough, and such appeals duly materialised. The German received and rejected a Roman ultimatum, and moved west towards the Sequanian fortress of Vesontio (Besançon). However, Caesar got there first. But then he was scandalised to discover that some of his junior officers, young upper-class Romans who had joined his staff to advance their careers, had worked themselves into a panic – because of the ferocity of their prospective German enemies. Or more probably – though he does not say so – they were influenced by the political opposition to Caesar in Rome, which was seeking to discredit every military operation he attempted.

A conference with Ariovistus, who knew all about this opposition, led to no result: which suited Caesar well, for he wanted a battle, and wanted it all the more since he was short of supplies. After an unsuccessful German raid on the smaller of his two camps, Caesar advanced with his six legions in triple line right up to the German camp, so that Ariovistus was 'compelled to lead his forces out' – which probably means that he, too, was running short of supplies.

Observing that the enemy's left wing showed signs of weakness, Caesar took command of the Roman right himself, and as the two

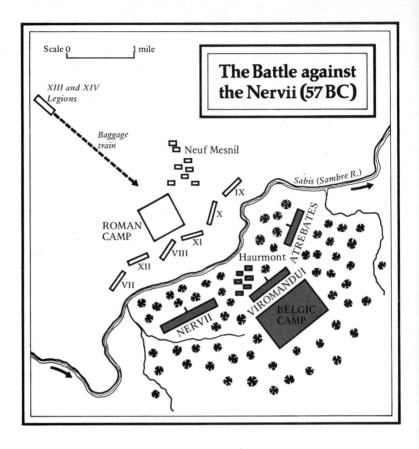

The Battle against the Nervii (57 BC)

armies simultaneously charged at one another with great violence, the legionaries dropped their javelins and fought hand to hand with their swords.

By quickly adopting their usual phalanx-formation the Germans were able to withstand the sword-thrusts, but many of our soldiers actually threw themselves on the wall of shields confronting them, wrenched the shields out of the enemy's hands, and stabbed them from above.

The Germans' left was thus routed, but their right began to press our troops hard by weight of numbers. Their perilous position attracted the attention of young Publius Crassus [son of the triumvir] who was in charge of the cavalry and better able to move about and see what was happening than those in the fighting line. He therefore sent up the third line to their relief.

This move turned the battle once more in our favour, and the enemy's whole army broke and fled without stopping until they came to the Rhine, some fifteen miles away. A very few of the strongest tried to swim the river, and a few others saved themselves by finding boats — including Ariovistus, who had the luck to come across a small craft moored to the

bank. All the rest were hunted down and killed by our cavalry. Ariovistus'
two wives perished in the flight ...

Caesar had completed two important campaigns in a single summer.

(Caesar, Gallic War, I, 52–4)

Ariovistus escaped, but he was a broken man, and died shortly
afterwards. Only three German tribes were permitted to stay west
of the Rhine, and the rest were forced back onto the opposite side.
There was no further trouble from this area for many years.

A coin of the Atrebates.

Rome, preoccupied and paralysed by street fighting among groups
of politically opposed gangsters, was not as impressed by these
spectacular victories as it might have been. But they had whetted
Caesar's appetite for even larger triumphs. And so he now turned
his attention towards north-eastern France, in which the dominant
peoples were Celticised Germans comprising the Belgic tribes. At
first the Belgae had been content to see the Helvetii and Ariovistus
defeated. But when Caesar established his winter quarters in
Gallic territory, it became increasingly clear that Gaul, far from
liberated from foreign invaders, was likely to acquire the latest
of them as a permanent incubus. In consequence, the Belgae now
began to mobilise their huge forces against him, and it was said
that they were massing together as many as 300,000 men. This
caused Caesar to rejoice, since he now saw a great vision of
conquering the whole of Gaul. With this immense prospect in
mind, he once again raised two new legions in Cisalpine Gaul, thus
bringing his total to eight, which was double the total originally
allotted to his command.

Then he set out and marched northwards as far as the River
Aisne – only to find that the main Belgic army had completely and
ludicrously fallen apart, because of the utter lack of the supply
services needed to keep such a large force in the field. This meant
that Caesar was able to deal with the tribes piecemeal, and reduce
them to subjection one by one. However, the most powerful of the
Belgic peoples, the Nervii of Hainault and Flanders who possessed
exceptionally formidable infantry, had kept out of this general
process of disintegration. It was they, therefore, whom Caesar
confronted, moving his army up to the River Sambre. But the
Roman intelligence and reconnaissance services had failed to
disclose the proximity of the Nervian army in a thick wood, from
which they now dashed out, sweeping the disorganised Roman
cavalry back over the river, and racing up the slope of the hill on
which the legionaries had not yet finished constructing their camp.

And Caesar goes on to offer a general's comment on one of the most hazardous battles he ever fought.

The soldiers were so pushed for time by the enemy's eagerness to fight that they could not even take the covers off their shields or put on helmets – not to speak of fixing on crests or decorations. Each man, on coming down from his work at the camp, went into action under the first standard he happened to see, so as not to waste time searching for his own unit ...

The legions were facing different ways and fighting separate actions, and the thick hedges obstructed their view. The result was that Caesar could not fix upon definite points for stationing reserves or foresee what would be needed in each part of the field, and unity of command was impossible.

(Caesar, *Gallic War*, II, 21–2)

In such adverse circumstances, continues Caesar, there were naturally ups and downs of fortune. At one moment the situation looked encouraging enough. For two legions on the left wing, after hurling their javelins, successfully charged the tribe of the Atrebates (allies of the Nervii), drove them back over the river, and chased them up a slope on the following side. The Roman centre also broke through. But this left the two legions on the right wing in perilous isolation, and when subjected to a violent onslaught they wavered and nearly broke.

As the situation was critical and no reserves were available, Caesar snatched a shield from a soldier in the rear [he did not have his own shield with him], made his way into the front line, addressed each centurion by name, and shouted encouragement to the rest of the troops, ordering them to push forward and open out their ranks, so that they could use their swords more easily.

(*Ibid.*, 25)

At this juncture, fortunately, two reserve legions arrived. Left in the rear to guard the baggage train, they had received news of the critical situation; and now they appeared over the brow of a neighbouring hill. At the same time, too, Caesar's principal lieutenant Labienus made a decisive intervention. Earlier on, leading the tenth legion, he had crossed the Sambre and captured the Nervian camp – and now he recrossed the river and took the enemy in the rear. Desperately fighting still, the Nervian infantry fought in vain, and its annihilation was only a matter of time. And so the battle came to its bloody end. Caesar had won yet another victory, and exulted (with some over-statement) that the name of the tribe was almost blotted off the face of the earth.

Meanwhile a legion commanded by Publius Crassus, the younger son of the triumvir, had been operating in north-west Gaul against the Veneti and other tribes of Brittany, and they duly offered their submission. 'These various operations', declared Caesar, 'had brought about a state of peace throughout Gaul.' This was scarcely an exaggeration, for it already seemed as if all resistance was at an end. The areas overrun by Caesar had not yet, it is true, been formally annexed as a new province, or as an extension of the already existing Narbonese province in the south. But Caesar believed that Roman suzerainty had been extended over all the tribes of the country, including the Belgic confederations of the north. After only two seasons of military operations, Gaul looked like a thoroughly conquered country.

The plunder taken had been immense, and such portions of these riches as had filtered through to Rome were producing a more favourable reaction towards the conqueror. Pompey proposed a thanksgiving of unprecedented duration, and even Cicero was prepared to second the proposal. This was out of gratitude not to Caesar but to Pompey, for although the latter had done nothing to prevent Cicero's exile, he had at least brought him back home again – and had taken Cicero's brother Quintus on his own staff.

Nevertheless, relations between the triumvirs themselves were no longer as harmonious as they had been before. For one thing, Pompey could not fail to feel pangs of jealousy about Caesar's victories, which were already being compared to his own conquests in the east. Furthermore, Clodius had begun to pronounce sharp attacks against Pompey: and Pompey believed that the instigator of this unfriendly attitude was Crassus. Cicero tried to take advantage of these strains between the triumvirs in the hope of widening the gaps between them still further. But the result proved exactly the opposite to what he had intended, for, on reflection, each one of the leaders concluded that he still needed the help of the other two. And so they decided in April 56 BC to come together, all three of them, and hold a conference. Since Caesar, if he had ventured to set foot within the borders of Italy, would have lost the indispensable immunity from prosecution which he possessed as governor, the meeting was held at Luca (Lucca), which at that time was situated within his own province of Cisalpine Gaul, just outside Italian territory.

At this conference it was agreed between the three triumvirs that steps should be taken, at the appropriate moment, to bestow upon each of them, by due process of law, what he most desired in order to fulfil his immediate ambitions. Crassus, restless because of the military successes of his two colleagues, was given a command against the only substantial power confronting Rome anywhere in the world, the Parthian empire which lay beyond the Euphrates. He and Pompey were to become consuls in 55 BC. Pompey was also awarded the rich provinces of Spain for five years – and, what is more, he was permitted to govern them *in absentia* through subordinates, while he himself remained near Rome and virtually controlled its government. Caesar's command was likewise renewed for a five-year duration, so that he could complete the exploitation of his provinces and undertake other projects beyond their frontiers. And Cicero was silenced: because although his brother Quintus soon left Pompey's service, he only did so in order to accept a transfer to the service of Caesar instead.

Since Caesar believed Gaul to be pacified, he now proposed, at long last, to turn his intention once again to the Illyrian section of his command, which likewise seemed to offer opportunities for cross-border aggression.

However, it immediately became clear, contrary to all expectations, that Gaul was not by any means pacified after all. The first trouble came from the Veneti of western Brittany, whose submission had been received in the previous year. They were a maritime people with a powerful fleet, who held a monopoly of the importation of tin and other products from the independent island of Britain. They had recently heard rumours that Caesar was planning an invasion of Britain – which would destroy their lucrative control of that country's trade. This news inspired them to think again about their recent submission; and they were further stimulated to do so by the strained relations between the triumvirs before the conference of Luca, which made them feel they could act with impunity.

Thus encouraged, they and a group of associated seafaring tribes, when visited by a number of Roman requisitioning officers, took the grave step of placing them under arrest. The rumour about Caesar's British project was perfectly accurate, and he could not carry out the expedition in the face of hostility from the Veneti and their friends, since this would deny him the control of the English Channel. Moreover, he now realised that a single local rising could easily spread like wildfire, and spark off the general uprising that had recently been regarded as impossible. So these

Reconstruction of Caesar's bridge across the Rhine (55 BC).

enemies, or rather rebels as Caesar now felt justified in calling them, had to be reduced. Since the strongholds of the tribesmen were inaccessible from the land, naval action was essential, and he therefore arranged for a fleet to be constructed on the Loire. As for the Veneti, they believed that the Roman armies and fleets could not stay long in their neighbourhood owing to the absence of grain, and decided in consequence upon a policy of economic attrition.

Sending subordinates far and wide in Gaul to overawe the other tribes and prevent them from joining up with the Veneti, Caesar entrusted one of his young officers, Decimus Brutus Albinus, with the command of the naval force that was to proceed against them, while he himself, quickly returning all the way from Illyricum, advanced into Brittany with a land army. Decimus Brutus at first found that the heavy oak vessels of the Veneti, which had leather sails strong enough to endure Atlantic gales, and unusually flat keels to avoid damage from shoals when the tide was out, were too

74

formidable for his relatively light Roman warships. Moreover, in spite of Caesar's land operations in which several strongholds were captured, it was clear – although the land-centred Romans never liked such a conclusion – that the decision had to come at sea. The scene of this engagement was in Quiberon Bay, and Caesar gives a lucid description of its unusual features.

Decimus Brutus and his officers knew that no injury could be inflicted on the enemy by ramming and when they tried erecting turrets they found that they were still overtopped by the foreigners' lofty sterns and were too low to make their missiles carry properly, while the enemy's fell with great force.

One device, however, that our men had prepared proved very useful – pointed hooks fixed into the ends of long poles, not unlike the grappling hooks used in sieges. With these the halyards were grasped and pulled taut, and then snapped by rowing hard away. This of course brought the yards down, and since the Gallic ships depended wholly on their sails and rigging, when stripped of these they were at once immobilised.

75

The Roman Forum: on the left are the
foundations of Caesar's Basilica Julia.

After that it was a soldiers' battle, in which the Romans easily proved superior, especially as it was fought under the eyes of Caesar and the whole army, so that any act of special bravery was bound to be noticed: all the cliffs and hills that commanded a near view of the sea were occupied by the troops ...

(Caesar, Gallic War, III, 14–5)

The battle was won, and the Gallic leaders executed, while the rest of the population were sold as slaves. Expeditions to Normandy and Aquitania by subordinates of Caesar were equally successful, and then he himself, in preparation for his British expedition, moved up to the marshy forest land on the Straits of Dover: though he found it impossible to stay there long, owing to the torrential downpours of rain that his army encountered.

Meanwhile at Rome, obedient henchmen had pushed through the laws granting the triumvirs the powers they had agreed to take at the conference of Luca. Although there was rioting, in which four lives were lost and a senator suffered a wound from the hand of Crassus himself, the measures were helped through by a thousand of Caesar's soldiers, whom he had conveniently allowed to go to Rome for their leave. He himself had continued to watch the situation in the capital from Cisalpine Gaul, where as usual he had established his winter headquarters. But then, early in spring 55 BC, he set off to cross the Alps for the fourth of his annual campaigns.

His first action was to throw back a German migration from the east, as he had already done three years earlier. This time, two large German tribes, the Usipetes and Tencteri, had crossed the Rhine in an enormous horde, including their wives and children, and when Caesar fell on them they fled. His account of what ensued is one of the most chilling passages in ancient literature.

When they reached the confluence of the Moselle and the Rhine, they realised that they could flee no farther. A large number were killed, and the rest plunged into the water and perished, overcome by the force of the current in their terror-stricken and exhausted state. The Romans returned to camp without a single fatal casualty, and with only a few wounded, although a grim struggle had been anticipated against an enemy four hundred and thirty thousand strong.

(Caesar, Ibid., IV, 15)

The dead probably did not number as many as 430,000. But they were evidently very numerous indeed.

3 Britain Twice Invaded and Abandoned

NOT LONG AFTERWARDS, Caesar carried out two enterprises which took him beyond the uttermost frontiers of Gaul. The first was a crossing of the Rhine, in order to support his allies on the other side of the river, and help them to overawe their enemies. However, to use his own words, 'a crossing by means of boats seemed to him both too risky, and beneath his dignity as a Roman commander'. Accordingly, within the short space of ten days, a trestle bridge fifteen hundred feet long and forty feet wide was constructed to span the river. Never had such a bridge been built before, and never had the bridging of so formidable a stream been attempted. It was a notable achievement of that magnificent engineering expertise which is one of the ancient Roman talents inherited by the modern Italians.

However, Caesar only spent eighteen days on the farther bank of the Rhine. This was not nearly long enough to produce any permanent results. Yet the gesture was a highly significant one, not only as propaganda to impress the barbarians, but because it explicitly rejected any idea that the ultimate limits of Roman power were to stop at the Rhine. On the contrary, Caesar was giving notice that they were extended into the indefinite distance.

In the same year, he launched another spectacular project that presented even greater technical difficulties, his first invasion of Britain. This involved not only the crossing of a mere river, however wide and impressive, but the embarkation upon a sea that lay beyond the uttermost extremity of the known world.

The reasons for invading Britain were various. Caesar himself attributes his decision to a desire to gain information about the country, which he was unable to acquire from any of the traders who visited it, or from other inhabitants of Gaul, or even from reconnaissance parties which he himself had sent across the English Channel. He was also eager to lay hands on the alleged wealth of the country, including its gold, silver and tin; and Britain was especially famous (beyond its merits) for pearls. He was also concerned to suppress the large numbers of Belgae who, after crossing from Gaul during the past decades, now led important tribal confederations in south-east England – and had supported his own Gallic enemies. Annexation may not necessarily have been in his mind. All round the frontiers of the empire there was a fringe of states and tribes which, although formally independent, in reality stood in various degrees of political or military or economic dependence upon Rome. It was into this complex

PREVIOUS PAGES Roman standards; the central one is the Eagle (*aquila*) of a legion.

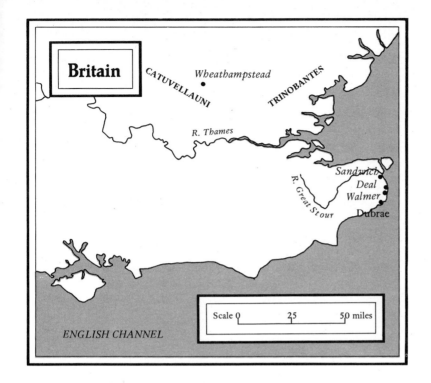

Britain

CATUVELLAUNI
Wheathampstead
TRINOBANTES
R. Thames
R. Great Stour
Sandwich
Deal
Walmer
Dubrae

Scale 0   25   50 miles

ENGLISH CHANNEL

system of 'client' states and protectorates that Caesar hoped to draw the confederacies and tribes of southern Britain.

However, owing to his crossing of the Rhine, he was not able to make a start until the time of year which, according to our present calendar, would be mid-July. Without waiting for his cavalry, which had failed to reach him on schedule, he transported two legions across the Channel, in eighty ships. Leaving Portus Itius (probably Gesoriacum, which is now Boulogne) in the middle of the night, the fleet was off Dubrae (Dover) about nine hours later. But this first attempt by the Romans to land in Britain was fraught with formidable problems. To begin with, the first landing place had to be abandoned, because it was too vulnerable to enemy javelins. So the fleet moved on, until it came to a point somewhere near Walmer or Deal. But the British had sent cavalry and chariots, and the landing was only effected after considerable difficulties. The legionaries, though somewhat daunted by this unfamiliar experience, finally managed to establish a beach head, and then drove their native assailants back, but the absence of cavalry prevented them from launching an effective pursuit. Nevertheless, the nearest British tribes were sufficiently cowed (or so it appeared)

81

A British helmet of bronze, probably first century BC.

to sue for peace. But Caesar now had a more formidable enemy to cope with.

On the fourth day after his arrival in Britain, the eighteen transports on which the cavalry had been embarked sailed from the northern port before a gentle breeze. When they were approaching Britain and were visible from the camp, such a violent storm suddenly arose that none of them could hold its course. Some were driven back to their starting-point; others, at great peril, were swept westwards to the south of the island. In spite of the danger they cast anchor, but as they were being filled with water by the waves, they were forced to stand out to sea into the darkness of night and return to the continent.

It happened to be full moon that night, at which time the Atlantic tides are particularly high – a fact unknown to the Romans. The result was that the warships used in the crossing, which had been beached, were water-logged, and the transports, which were riding at anchor, were knocked about by the storm, without the soldiers having any chance of interfering to save them. A number of ships were shattered, and the rest, having lost their cables, anchors, and the remainder of their tackle, were unusable, which naturally threw the whole army into great consternation. For they had no other vessels in which they could return, nor any materials for repairing the fleet. And since it had been generally understood that they were to return to Gaul for the winter, they had not provided themselves with a stock of grain for wintering in Britain.

(Caesar, Gallic War, IV, 28–9)

This disaster to the fleet encouraged the British chieftains to rally, and they launched an ambush against one of the legions that was foraging. Caesar came to its rescue, and when the British attacked his camp he put them to flight. After this, they requested peace once again, and Caesar, after doubling the number of hostages they must provide, agreed. Then he and his army returned to Gaul.

He admitted that the tribes sent nothing like the number of hostages they had promised, and it is doubtful whether any of the required tribute had been paid at all. Nevertheless, Roman might had been displayed in an almost mythical land separated from the continent by the Ocean itself: and Roman public opinion was stirred. True, Pompey could later suggest that the Channel was merely a mud-flat. Yet, at the time, almost the only derogatory remarks came from Cato, who took this opportunity to remind the senate of Caesar's cruelty towards the Germans in the earlier part of the year, stating that his attack upon their tribes women and children and all, had taken place during a truce, and therefore constituted a breach of religious faith. But Caesar answered angrily, and the protest attracted little support. On the contrary, the senate voted him a thanksgiving in unprecedentedly eulogistic language. In political terms, his spectacular enterprises were beginning to yield results.

Early in 54 BC, he proceeded to Illyricum, and his presence brought a number of recalcitrant tribesmen to heel. But it was not his intention to remain in this sector of his command. For he was eager to proceed to Britain for a second time, in the hope of securing more permanent results – possibly, this time, the annexation of the whole island. Yet he could not start off immediately, because it first seemed imperative to overcome the powerful eastern tribe of the Treviri, whose capital was the city now called Trier on the Moselle. They had failed to attend meetings to which Caesar had summoned them, and their cavalry was the most powerful in Gaul; so Caesar took four legions to improve their state of mind.

With Rome's chief ally the Aedui, too, there was trouble, since the leader of its nationalist faction refused to accept an invitation to cross the Channel with Caesar, who consequently sent a cavalry detachment to cut him down.

In view of these difficulties, and because of adverse winds, his second expedition to Britain, though it started about four weeks earlier than in the previous year, was again rather too late in the season. But finally he set sail from Portus Itius once more. This time he took with him five legions and 2,000 cavalry, carried on 800 transports, including 200 contributed by private Roman financiers in exchange for a share of the eventual loot. This was a larger fleet than the Channel was ever to see again for very nearly two thousand years – in fact, until 1944. Tackle especially devised to meet British conditions was taken aboard, and the decks were made unusually low, in order to facilitate unloading.

The ships sailed round to the shores of east Kent, and disembarked at a point in the region of Sandwich. They arrived at about mid-day, and the landing of the troops lasted until long after darkness had fallen. The British tribes of the region did not venture to oppose the disembarkation, but their army, for the time being, stood well out of sight. Eager to march against them as soon as possible, Caesar did not beach his ships, but left them riding in anchor on the sandy shore, with a legionary force standing guard. Then without further delay, although it was already after midnight, he marched the rest of his army twelve miles inland as far as the Great Stour, where a first successful engagement was fought. It was followed up by a rapid pursuit. But while this was still under way, Caesar received news that history had repeated itself. For there had been a great storm in the night, he now learnt, which had totally destroyed forty of his ships and severely damaged most of the rest. Returning hastily to the coast, he extracted every skilled workman out of the ranks to start on repairs, and at once sent to Gaul for an additional supply of expert labour – and for additional ships as well. He also decided, rather belatedly, to beach his own remaining ships, and spent ten days building a fortification to protect them from attacks. Then, finally, he proceeded inland once again.

Meanwhile, the British tribes set aside their feuds for the time being, and appointed Cassivellaunus of the Catuvellauni, a tribe centred upon Hertfordshire, as their commander-in-chief. Encountering stiff opposition as he marched against him, Caesar found that the British tactics presented difficult problems.

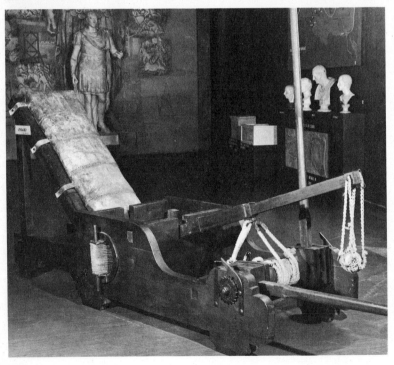

OPPOSITE TOP Roman siege machinery: the 'ram' (*aries*); BOTTOM the 'wild ass' (*onager*); BELOW the 'tortoise' (*testudo*).

Ancient British art: RIGHT The Aylesford bucket; from pre-Roman Britain.
BOTTOM RIGHT Electrum torque from the Snettisham treasure.

It was seen that our troops were too heavily weighed by their armour to deal with such an enemy. They could not pursue them when they retreated, and dared not get separated from their standards. The cavalry, too, found it very dangerous work fighting the charioteers. For the Britons would generally give ground on purpose, and after drawing them some distance from the legions would jump down from their chariots and fight on foot, with the odds in their favour. In engaging their cavalry our men were not much better off: their tactics were such that the danger was exactly the same for pursuers and pursued. A further difficulty was that they never fought in close order, but in very open formation, and had reserves posted here and there. In this way, the various groups covered one another's retreat, and fresh troops replaced those who were tired.

(Caesar, *Gallic War*, v, 16)

Nevertheless, Caesar pressed on, and in spite of losses managed to force his way across the Thames at its only fordable point. The enemy were compelled to recoil further into the interior, and before long their commander, as Caesar tells us, wisely abandoned any idea of fighting a pitched battle, instead launching ambushes and guerilla actions under cover of the forests.

Nevertheless the Roman force, encouraged by the collaboration of the strong Trinobantes of Essex, pressed ahead and destroyed Cassivellaunus' fortified capital, which was probably at Wheathampstead, north of St Albans. Cassivellaunus himself, however, escaped and sent letters to four Kentish chieftains ordering them to attack Caesar's camp. As requested, they delivered a surprise assualt on the camp, but their onslaught was beaten off. Thereupon Cassivellaunus asked for terms, and since Caesar had decided it was unwise to risk a winter in Britain, he agreed to the proposed conditions. Hostages were delivered, an annual tribute was fixed, and the return voyage was successfully effected in two journeys.

Very little tribute, however, was actually paid. In other words, Caesar's plans to maintain the British tribes as 'client' dependents came to nothing. The Romans never, at any time, succeeded in conquering the entire island – and another whole century was to pass before even the southern part of England became Roman territory. If Caesar himself, at the beginning of 54 BC, had contemplated annexation, the idea was no longer in his mind by the end of the year. Cicero asked his brother, who was on Caesar's staff, to write an epic poem describing the conquered island. But the poem was never forthcoming. And even the loot fell considerably short of expectations. As the *Commentaries* scarcely conceal, Britain was one of the few failures of Caesar's career.

OPPOSITE The Alps, crossed time and time again by Caesar and his army, in their effort to subdue the rebellious Gallic tribes.

4 The Great Gallic Rebellion

WHILE CAESAR WAS IN BRITAIN for the second time he planned, on returning to Gaul, to split up his army, and send it into winter quarters in a number of widely distributed parts of the country. This was partly to prevent the food requirements of the troops from weighing too heavily on any one region. But security considerations were evidently in his mind as well, since he felt he needed garrisons in as many different centres as possible so as to minimise the danger of local revolts.

This precautionary attitude suggests that he was becoming more and more aware how far his previous assumption that Gaul was already a conquered country was at variance with the true facts. This had already become pretty clear by the autumn of 54 BC, when a critical situation developed among the Carnutes who dwelt in heavily wooded territory round Cenabum (Orléans). The Carnutes were particularly important because their country contained the principal meeting place of the Druids, religious leaders who exercised great influence throughout Gaul, largely controlling not only the civil and legal administration but the education of Gallic children as well. In 57 BC, Caesar had himself taken the trouble to choose a new king for the Carnutes: and now he learnt that his appointee had been murdered. He therefore detached a body of troops to deal with this situation, though he did not regard it as serious enough to necessitate a large scale convergence of troops, which would have meant abandoning his scheme for widely scattered winter quarters.

However, a much worse disaster was now to come, and from another region altogether. When Caesar had chosen the locations for the winter camps, he had concentrated them particularly thickly in north-eastern Gaul, because that was the home of the powerful Belgae. The farthest away of these garrisons, comprising one and a half legions consisting mostly of raw recruits, was at Aduatuca (Tongeren, north of Liège), and it was here that the blow fell. For Ambiorix, king of one of the smaller Belgic nations, the Eburones in the Ardennes, suddenly attacked the camp, and its defenders were massacred. The infection rapidly spread to other Belgic tribes, and Quintus Cicero at Samarobriva (Amiens), confronted with an army who used siege engines imitated from the Romans, was only with the greatest difficulty able to hold out until Caesar was in a position to relieve him. And meanwhile Caesar's principal deputy Labienus, near Sedan, was faced by a rebellion from the Treviri, which he dealt with by putting their principal chief to death.

By this time there was no doubt that the new Roman régime in
Gaul had collapsed in total ruin. After the loss of his legionaries at
Aduatuca, Caesar allowed his beard and hair to grow, asserting
that he would not cut them until he had taken vengeance on the
Gauls who had been responsible for the slaughter. And in the
following winter he did not follow his usual practice of crossing
the Alps, but spent the winter months near Samarobriva instead.
From there he ordered the recruitment of two new legions in
Cisalpine Gaul, and Pompey agreed to give him another which he
was himself in the process of mobilising: so that now, in spite of
the loss of Sabinus' troops, he had as many as ten legions at his
disposal.

During the first months of 53 BC, he called a meeting of Gallic
chieftains at Samarobriva, and subsequently moved with all the
delegates to Lutetia (Paris), in order to be in closer proximity to
the menacing Belgae. The various dissident tribes gave in, or were
liquidated. Ambiorix, who had destroyed the Roman garrison at
Aduatuca, escaped, but Caesar seized another disaffected Gallic
leader, Acco, prince of the Senones, and summoning a fresh
conference in the autumn at Durocortorum (Reims), put him to
death with horrifying brutality in front of all the representatives
of the other tribes.

As always, Caesar was keeping the closest possible eye on Rome,
through his numerous and effective agents, and by means of a

Caesar's siege works at
Avaricum (Bourges), 52 BC.

93

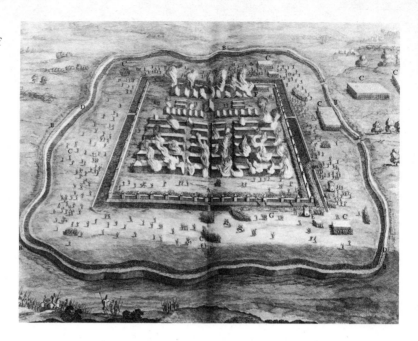

Reconstruction of the attack by the Nervii on the camp of Quintus Cicero.

massive correspondence. Although Pompey, while remaining governor of Spain *in absentia*, stayed in the neighbourhood of the capital, incessant disorders had virtually reduced its public life to chaos. Moreover, two deaths which now occurred made a decisive and ominous change in the balance of political power. First Julia, Pompey's wife and Caesar's daughter, had a difficult childbirth which proved fatal – so that the only personage who might have kept the two principal leaders on reasonably friendly terms with one another had been suddenly removed from the scene. Next, the colleague of these leaders, the third triumvir Crassus, met his end. As planned, he had departed from Italy and moved east, to fight against the Parthians; but after suffering a serious defeat at Carrhae (Haran) in northern Mesopotamia, he had gone to the enemy to negotiate, whereupon they put him to death. His elimination meant that an eventual direct confrontation between his surviving fellow triumvirs, Pompey and Caesar, had become a good deal likelier than before.

In 52 BC disorders in and around Rome became more and more serious, resulting finally in the violent death of one of their chief instigators, Clodius. In order to deal with the rising wave of disturbances, Pompey not only assumed his third consulship, but for some months held the office without a colleague. To what lengths his own ambitions ran remains disputable: but the men

94

who felt suspicious of him, who were numerous because of his tricky methods, easily succeeded in detecting autocratic intentions. This was certainly the view of Caesar's friends. Caesar himself, on the other hand, tried to patch up the alliance with Pompey once again, by proposing a new matrimonial compact. Offering to set aside his own wife Calpurnia, who was childless, he proposed to marry Pompey's daughter, while Pompey was to wed Caesar's grand-niece Octavia. But Pompey now took a significant political decision. Rejecting the suggested bargain, he instead married a young woman named Cornelia, who was the daughter of one of the loftiest pillars of Roman aristocratic society, Metellus Scipio. He also elevated Metellus Scipio to be his fellow-consul. These were clear indications that Pompey, outliving his reputation as an anti-senatorial rebel, was drawing nearer to the conservative senatorial cause – and was becoming less sympathetic, that is to say, towards Caesar.

And yet at the same time Pompey could not bring himself to alienate his colleague unnecessarily. For example, he showed respect for Caesar's constant anxiety about his future position in the state by deliberately taking steps to allay such worries. If Caesar was to preserve his career and perhaps his life from potential prosecutors, it was still as essential as ever that there should not be a gap between his present governorship and the next public office he would be able to assume. That could only be a second consul-ship, and according to the law he could not hold it until 48 BC, ten years after he had finished his first tenure of the same office. What Pompey obligingly did now, therefore, was to sponsor bills which would permit Caesar to stand for the consulship *in absentia* – thus relieving him from the necessity of vacating his command before winning and taking over that office. But at the same time the devious Pompey set in motion other legislation which looked as if he was taking away with one hand what he had granted with the other. Moreover, while leaving the terminal date of Caesar's governorship in the air, he arranged for his own absentee governor-ship of Spain to be extended for another five years. You could not put your finger on any actual disloyalty in this, but it was hardly reassuring to Caesar: and he was well aware that Pompey's advisers were always pressing him to go much further in the direction of unfriendliness, and indeed to make an open break.

Meanwhile, it had become clear to an increasing number of Gauls that Caesar was planning nothing less than the permanent annexation of their country. At the same time, the disturbances at

Vercingetorix.

Rome encouraged them to make a further and more determined attempt to resist this fate. It was at this point, therefore, that their uprisings ceased to be merely localised affairs and became a massive general revolt, involving a majority of all the tribes. The Carnutes, once more, were the people who took the initiative, when early in 52 BC they put a number of Romans to death.

However, the leaders of the great insurrection of 52 BC were not the Carnutes but the much more formidable tribe of the Arverni, whose nation, centred upon the Auvergne, was one of the greatest in Gaul. Their leader and guide, the hero of Frenchmen throughout the ages to come, was Vercingetorix – the only man the Gauls produced who had the talent and vision to cause a really serious disruption of Caesar's plans.

While spending the winter in Cisalpine Gaul once again, he learnt that serious trouble was on the way, and hastened northwards. The pass across the Cévennes was covered by six feet of snow, but Caesar had the road cleared in a day and a night, and appeared unexpectedly upon the Arvernian borders. Vercingetorix was now compelled to concentrate upon the defence of his homeland, but Caesar moved on with great rapidity into central Gaul, feeding his troops, of necessity, upon almost nothing but meat, which caused them considerable dissatisfaction. Vercingetorix decided that the only way to stop him was to destroy every Gallic settlement which might provide him with supplies; and the willingness of many tribesmen to accept this desperately painful measure was a tribute to his compelling leadership. One tribe alone, the Bituriges, burnt down nearly two dozen of their own towns and villages, but begged to be allowed to keep their capital Avaricum (Bourges), on the grounds that the strong situation of the place made it defensible. Vercingetorix, very reluctantly, agreed. But after a siege of three and a half weeks the Romans broke into the town, and out of its population of forty-thousand no more than eight hundred escaped massacre. Yet this catastrophe only served to increase the rebel leader's prestige still further, since it showed his policy of destruction had been right.

Coin of the Aedui.

Moving his headquarters to Noviodunum (Nevers), which belonged to Rome's traditional but now wobbling ally the Aedui, Caesar decided that the rapid and widespread extension of the revolt made it necessary for him to divide his army into two major sections. So Labienus was sent northwards towards Lutetia (Paris), the capital of the tribe of the Parisii, while Caesar himself moved against the chief fortress of the Arverni themselves, Gergovia, a few miles from the modern city of Clermont-Ferrand. His men attacked the walls impetuously, but suffered a serious setback, in which more than seven hundred legionaries, including forty-six centurions, were lost. This compelled Caesar to break off the siege. On the receipt of this news, the Aedui finally decided to join the insurgents, and massacred all the Romans at Noviodunum, seizing their stores and destroying surplus grain. Then they demolished the whole town, and the Parisii too, in order to thwart Labienus, burnt Lutetia to the ground. At this point Caesar regarded it as unsafe to operate with two separate armies any longer, and succeeding in effecting a junction with Labienus: whereupon their combined column, relying on the excellent German cavalry that Caesar now possessed, beat off a dangerous three-pronged charge by the Gauls, inflicting heavy losses. Vercingetorix, who had led the unsuccessful attack, fell back into his fortress of Alesia (Alise-Sainte-Reine) on the lofty, isolated plateau of Mont-Auxois. Before barricading himself inside its walls, however, he sent all his cavalry away, with the dual purpose of diminishing his supply problem and enabling the horsemen to

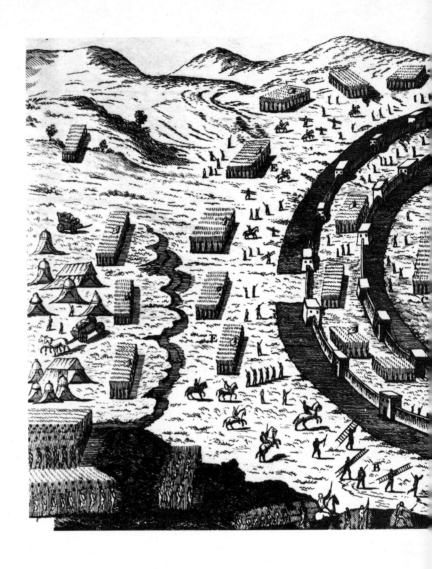

ABOVE Reconstruction of the siege of Alesia, 52 BC. RIGHT Aerial photograph of Alise-Sainte-Reine, on the site of ancient Alesia.

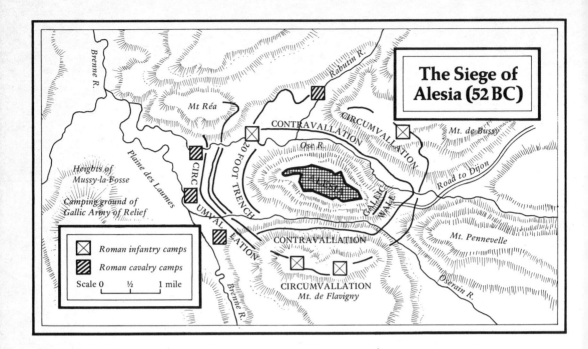

The Siege of
Alesia (52 BC)

Roman infantry camps
Roman cavalry camps
Scale 0   ½   1 mile

raise a relief force from the tribes round about. Caesar, an expert at
the traditional Roman military art of entrenchment, encircled the
town by four lines of fortifications, of which the innermost was
ten miles in circumference, and the outermost fourteen. This
multiplicity of fortified lines meant that his troops, when the
Gauls sent their reinforcements, would be able to face inwards and
outwards at the same time. In due course the Gallic relief force
arrived. Caesar estimated it at a quarter of a million infantry and
eight thousand cavalry, contributed by forty-three tribes, and
although he was probably exaggerating, there is no doubt that
they sent an enormous mass of men and horses. For four long days,
the Romans survived a simultaneous attack from both directions:
and then, finally, Labienus concluded that the moment had come
to strike the relieving army a decisive blow. Caesar himself took
command of a force of eleven cohorts (that is to say rather more
than a legion, which was ten cohorts strong) and the attack was a
complete success.

The Gallic relief army was routed, and its soldiers slaughtered
or dispersed. It had completely failed to achieve its purpose.
Indeed, owing to its huge size, large portions of it had never been
engaged: and in any case its supply problems were insuperable.
For Vercingetorix the end had come, and he surrendered, to

100

remain a captive until his execution six years later; Napoleon III built him a monument on the site of his final defeat.

The Great Revolt had been stamped out. With hindsight, it seems badly timed, because if the rising could have been postponed for two or three years its outbreak would have coincided with a Roman civil war. Besides, many of the formidable Belgic tribes had contributed too little and too late. In 51 BC, after the main rebellion was over, Caesar proceeded against two of them, and then crossed almost the whole length of Gaul to the Dordogne, in order to chase a host of recalcitrant southerners into the hill-fortress of Uxello-dunum (Puy d'Issolu). There they were overwhelmed by the Romans, and all survivors, if they had carried arms, had their hands cut off.

This was the last of many ruthless atrocities perpetuated by Caesar in the name of pacification. The Gallic War was now at an end, and he himself claimed that he had fought more than thirty pitched battles, captured over eight hundred towns, and fought against between three and four million men, of whom he had captured a million and slain a million more. Like other figures published by Caesar, and indeed like communiqués of enemy casualty figures at every period of history, these statistics must be regarded with scepticism. All the same the losses of the Gauls were terrible. Their country owed its collapse to the persistent failure of its peoples to become truly united – for even the measure of unity attained by Vercingetorix had only been partial and precarious. And so this very large territory was duly conquered and annexed, and was now assessed for tribute. In the process, the whole concept and character of the Roman empire had been transformed. It was no longer the purely Mediterranean empire which it had been up to now, but an empire of continental and northern Europe as well.

When allowance is made for an inevitable element of self-praise, the picture of Caesar as a general which his own *Commentaries* delineate does not need a great deal of qualification. That he was one of the supreme commanders of all time is obvious. But controversy has raged between those who maintain that he was a highly original general, and others who prefer to regard him as a commander who skilfully utilised, and perfected, a machine he had inherited from others. The truth lies somewhere between the two views. He knew all there was to know about the army he had taken over, but he also left his own stamp on every aspect of its operations and organisation. His own greatest personal merits were speed, timing, and flexibility in the face of suddenly changing circumstances. Furthermore, his personal endurance was super-normal. A splendid horseman, who, as an alternative to riding, thought nothing of covering a hundred miles a day in a light carriage, on appalling roads – and all the while dictating official letters or literary works to his secretaries – he was breathtakingly quick in mind and movement alike: far too quick for his enemies.

Sometimes this rapidity landed him in alarming mistakes and crises, but he became accustomed to extricating himself and achieving victory by a hair's breadth. Time after time, all was successfully staked on a single throw: this was the luck for which he was so famous. His *Commentaries* pay respectful tribute to luck: but luck could and must be given a helping hand, and the odds harnessed in his own favour.

Reconstruction of the ballista, a Roman siege-engine.

Tower containing a battering-ram, for sieges.

Urging advantage he improved all odds,
And made the most of fortune and the gods.

(adapted from Lucan, Pharsalia, I, 149–50)

About the smart young men from Rome who joined his staff as officers, Caesar writes with a certain amount of scorn. But a more disappointing feature about the *Commentaries* is that even his best generals, and other senior officers, do not always seem to be given enough credit. This may have been partly due to the conventions of the Commentary form, but it may also owe something to Caesar's awareness that he himself was not quite as other men are – an awareness which may explain why, in the civil wars that were to follow, a number of commanders who had served him loyally in the Gallic campaigns decided to take the other side. Outstanding among those who were to take such a decision was his own deputy through the entire period of the operations in Gaul, Labienus – an exceedingly able general, with ideas about the uses of cavalry that were far in advance of his time.

Caesar also had a brilliant chief of staff, Mamurra, who, among many other duties, presided over Caesar's unnamed expert engineers. Like Labienus he made very large sums of money out of the Gallic War, and the elegant poet Catullus, who hated upstarts such as Mamurra and did not think much more highly of his distinguished employer either, wrote about him with the acutest distaste.

> What man could stomach the sight
> That was not enthralled
> By loot, lechery and the political game?
> Intolerable Mamurra
> Squanders
> What shaggy Gauls
> What ultimate Britons
> Once possessed. . . .
> Is this the reason
> Rome's topmost tycoons,
> Father and son-in-law,
> Have been playing billiards
> With our world?

(Catullus, 29)

All the same, senior officers like Mamurra, and a former muleteer named Publius Ventidius who managed the supply system of Caesar's army – men who came from the Italian townships and not from Rome – must have played an enormously valuable part during all those years in Gaul. Yet their commander's *Gallic War* tells us little enough of their vital problems, such as the provision of grain and other food, and the manufacture and distribution of uniforms and boots. However, Caesar is less grudging in his approbation of the centurions, those men of iron who combined, as we should see it, two roles in one, those of company commanders and very senior non-commissioned officers. The centurions were the natural leaders and spokesmen of the rank and file. Caesar was determined to win their personal loyalty, and he succeeded in his aim.

To the ordinary legionaries, he was bound fast in a brilliantly successful relationship to which almost every one of them responded with emotion. The strength of this magnetic bond emerges in a thousand ways from the *Commentaries*, and, although Caesar writes with a fond complacency on the subject, it is clear enough from the results that he was telling the truth. One of the finest orators of the day, he addressed his men continually and effectively. He shared their hardships and their perils, and in battle he was to be seen in the forefront and at the point of maximum danger. While battle-discipline was maintained at a rigorous level, at other times he was indulgent about discipline, turning a blind eye when the legionaries found an opportunity to drink and plunder. He also doubled their pay.

In response to all this, they felt much greater loyalty to himself than they felt to the state. The tendency for generals to capture the allegiance of their soldiers in this way had been increasing over the whole of the previous half century, while the old conscript system was gradually giving way to armies raised from volunteers. These volunteer soldiers expected their rewards, and particularly their land allotments after discharge, not from the government but from the commanders who had been leading them in battle: and this was one of the developments that precipitated the break-up of the Republic. Not every commander found himself in a position to satisfy their needs, especially since their satisfaction received so little sympathy from the senate. But Caesar could and did give them what they wanted – and indeed after the Gallic War, if the senate would not cooperate, he was able to act on his own account, since the loot of Gauls had made him, for the first time in his life, a very rich man indeed.

5 Shall Caesar

or Pompey Rule?

THROUGHOUT THE REVOLT OF VERCINGETORIX, Caesar was unable to maintain his habitual contacts with Rome, and Pompey used this opportunity to gain a good deal of political ground at his expense. But worse still, Pompey's elevation of Metellus Scipio to be his fellow-consul meant that the conservative right wing now regarded him as their ally, and that he himself, in growing fear of Caesar, had largely come to accept this novel situation. Among these diehards were formidable 'hawks' who wanted no sort of political accommodation between the two surviving triumvirs – men like the Claudii Marcelli, a family which now won three successive consulships and continuously promoted measures calculated to bring about Caesar's political destruction.

The most convincing of their arguments was that the Gallic War had now come to an end and no longer needed a general, so that Caesar must return to private life, the condition of mortal vulnerability that he was above all determined to avoid. Pompey, although still not wholeheartedly accepting this deliberately provocative approach, finally agreed, nevertheless, that the question of appointing Caesar's successor as governor might at least be considered and discussed by the senate: and for the purpose of this discussion a definite date was fixed, namely 1 March 50 BC. What might happen if Caesar flatly refused to give up his army until he was safely consul once again, Pompey declined to imagine. But in this whole matter he was carrying his famous powers of evasion to excessive lengths, since it must have been abundantly clear to him that Caesar would never accept the temporary retirement that was now being proposed.

Meanwhile Caesar, faced with this closing of the ranks against him, was doing his best to acquire valuable new supporters at Rome. One of the consuls of 51 BC, Paullus, after receiving a heavy bribe, became his friend. He also gained the services of a brilliant young man, Curio, one of the tribunes of the people for the following year, who in response to Caesar's offer to pay his enormous debts placed himself at his disposal. A steadfast tribune was of great value to a political leader, because he was able to veto unwelcome measures in the senate. And that is just what Curio did: during the spring and early summer of his year of office he persistently vetoed one demand after another that a successor to Caesar's command should be appointed. Curio also suggested, as a variant, that *both* Caesar *and* Pompey should resign – Caesar from his governorship of the two Gauls and Illyricum, and Pompey from his absentee governorship of Spain. This proposal attracted a large number of senators, the silent majority whose principal desire was to keep the peace. But a small group of diehards ensured its rejection.

At this juncture Pompey took to his bed, seriously ill. He managed to formulate a fresh plan for a compromise solution, but Caesar thought it contained a trap. When Pompey got better, the affectionate manifestations that greeted his recovery increased his confidence, and made him more willing than before to take a strong line. Accordingly, at the July elections, he supported two ultra-conservatives who were standing for the consulships of the following year, and they were duly elected. But at the same time Caesar secured the election of a tribune to carry on Curio's work: he was a nobleman distantly related to himself, the clever, flamboyant, courageous young Antony (Marcus Antonius).

While these developments were taking place, the orator Cicero was keenly watching each of them in turn from distant Asia Minor, where he had reluctantly gone to serve out a year's governorship of the province of Cilicia. He was kept well posted from Rome, and in September one of his most intelligent correspondents, Caelius, sent him a distinctly pessimistic prognosis.

The point at issue is this, and it is over this that the men in power are going to fight: Pompey has made up his mind not to let Caesar be elected consul without his first surrendering army and provinces, while Caesar is convinced that his personal security depends on his keeping his army ... So their old love-affair and their detestable alliance have not decayed into furtive bickering but have erupted into open war.

(Cicero, *Letters to Friends*, VIII, 14)

However, before the year was out, Curio made yet another attempt at reconciling the protagonists. The more ferocious members of the senate were still continuing to canvass bellicose measures, and were now attracting a good deal of agreement. Yet somehow or other Curio now persuaded the senators to agree, by a very large majority, to his earlier proposal that both Caesar and Pompey should lay down their commands at the same time. But whether Caesar would maintain his objection to this idea was never put to the test, for the motion was vetoed. Then, on the very next day, the consul Gaius Marcellus, with the support of both the consuls designate for the next year, called on Pompey to assume command of all the forces of the Republic. Pompey accepted the commission, adding the largely formal reservation 'unless a better way can be found', and took charge of two legions which were destined for Syria but had not yet departed.

Roman bridge of late
Republican date near
Asculum (Ascoli Piceno).

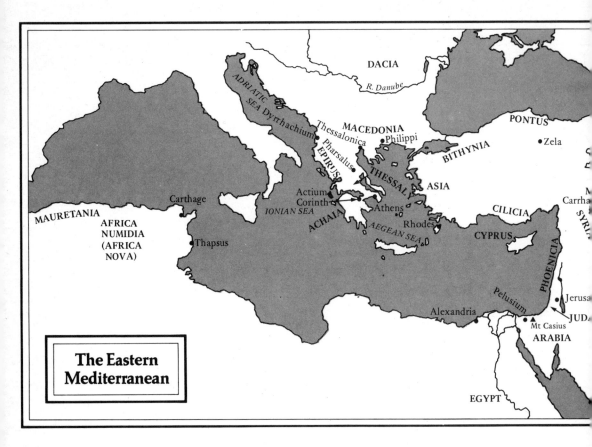

The Eastern Mediterranean

Negotiations between the two sides continued. But when Caesar, who was now near the south-eastern border of his Cisalpine province, sent a fresh message to the senate, the new tribune, Antony, supported by one of his colleagues, could scarcely gain a hearing to read it out, and the senators now proceeded to pass an emergency decree requesting, in traditional terms, that all principal officials should come to the defence of the state. Before this crisis measure was approved, Antony and his associate were warned to depart from Rome, since after the decree came into force they would be liable to forcible coercion. And so they hastened north, on their way to join Caesar and his army.

The fatal moment had come. On the night of 10 January 49 BC (the calendar was seven weeks in advance of the seasons), Caesar, accompanied by a single legion, crossed the Rubicon, an insignificant stream, now called the Fiumicino, which formed the border between Cisalpine Gaul and Italy. When he moved across the bridge, Caesar was deliberately breaking Rome's law of treason

forbidding governors to take their armies outside their provinces – a law which Sulla had formulated precisely with the purpose of curbing such over-ambitious commanders. Suetonius describes how the decisive step was taken.

When word came that the veto of the tribunes had been set aside and that they themselves had left the city, he at once sent on a few cohorts with all secrecy, and then, to disarm suspicion, concealed his purpose by appearing at a public show, inspecting the plans of a gladiatorial school which he intended building, and joining as usual in a banquet with a large number of other people. It was not until after sunset that he set out very secretly with a small company, taking the mules from a baker's shop nearby and harnessing them to a carriage; and when his lights went out and he lost his way, he was astray for some time, but at last found a guide at dawn and got back to the road on foot by narrow by-paths.

Then, overtaking his cohorts at the river Rubicon, which was the boundary of his province, he paused for a while, and realising what a step he was taking he turned to those about him and said: 'Even now we may draw back: but once cross that little bridge, and the whole issue is with the sword.'

(Suetonius, *Divus Julius*, 31)

The same account predictably continues with the appearance of a miraculous spectre, which inspired Caesar's decision to take the irreparable step. There was also a tradition that, as he crossed, he described what he was doing in a gambler's phraseology, declaring that the die was now cast, or, according to another account, crying out: *Let the dice fly high!*

The best way, however, to make the dice fall aright was to take adequate precautions, and this Caesar had done. For he had summoned up two legions and twenty-two new cohorts from Gaul, while leaving three legions in the south of that country in case of an attack from Pompey's forces in Spain. And now he himself pressed forward into central Italy, dividing his own small force into two columns, one heading for Arretium (Arezzo) and the other, led by himself, making for Ariminum (Rimini), where it was joined by the two friendly tribunes from Rome.

The opposing conservative leaders were in disarray, differing in their ideas of what should be done; but they were united in their jealousy of Pompey and refusal to allow him the powers he needed to act effectively as commander-in-chief. Furthermore, his and their intelligence had been gravely at fault, for they totally underestimated Caesar's capacity to launch an invasion of Italy.

This erroneous assessment had largely been due to Pompey's own over-optimism about the support the Italian municipalities would give him. But his conservative associates, too, had derived excessive confidence from the adherence of virtually all the ex-consuls and other senior senators to their cause, in addition to Labienus and others of Caesar's former generals. However, in military terms, the ex-consuls were of very little value: and Caesar's ex-generals, though more talented, were still not so good as Caesar himself. His invasion of Italy enjoyed a lightning success. One township after another opened its gates; and Pompey retreated southwards, towards Capua in Campania. The consuls for the year, who had remained in Rome up to now, proceeded to evacuate the city, and did so with such precipitancy that the reserve treasury in the Temple of Saturn was left behind. At Corfinium (near Pentima, almost due east of Rome) was the great and wealthy nobleman Ahenobarbus, with a considerable force. Pompey requested him to retire and effect a junction with his own army, but Ahenobarbus, who mortally hated Caesar, decided to make a stand. Very soon, however, his resistance collapsed (21 February), and Caesar had the fifty senators and knights of his entourage, including Ahenobarbus himself, brought before him. Then came a political sensation, for he allowed them all to go free. From the man who had massacred countless Germans and Gauls, this clemency towards Romans was something new.

The two principal henchmen whom Caesar had left to fill the vacuum in Rome, the knights Gaius Oppius and Lucius Balbus, evidently wrote congratulating him on this merciful policy. And Caesar, in a letter intended for wider circulation, replied in these terms:

> I am glad to know from your letter that you approve strongly of what happened at Corfinium ... Let us see if we cannot win everybody over by such means, and so achieve a victory which is more than ephemeral. History proves that by practising cruelty you earn nothing but hatred. Nobody has ever achieved a lasting victory by such methods except Sulla, and Sulla is a man whom I do not propose to imitate. Why should this not be our new Programme for Victory? Why should we not arm ourselves with compassion and generosity as our weapons?
>
> (Cicero, *Letters to Atticus*, IX, 7c)

Ancient plan showing the Theatre of Pompey, near the spot where Caesar was murdered.

And Caesar proceeded to reinforce this propagandist measure by composing the second part of his *Commentaries*, the *Civil War*, in which he describes the fighting against Pompey in this year and

114

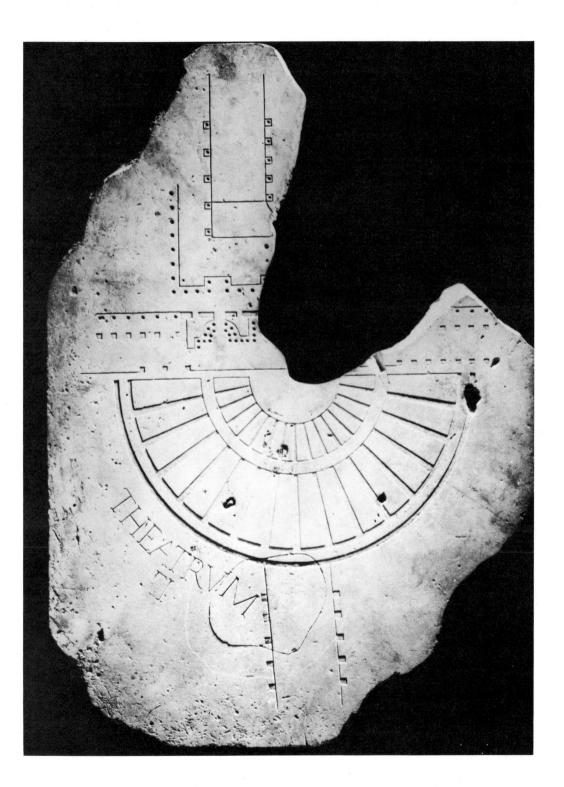

the next, while disparaging, whenever opportunity arose, the motives of his enemies.

Some, however, reproached Caesar for a course of action which would only set Ahenobarbus and the other distinguished ex-prisoners free so that they could immediately start fighting against him again (and indeed that is precisely what happened). But Caesar replied with a famous Olympian remark: 'There is nothing which I so much covet as that I should be like myself, and they like themselves'. And four hundred years later he was still remembered for another comment as well, that 'the recollection of cruelty is a wretched support of old age'.

The impression made by his clemency at Corfinium was profound. Indeed, even Cicero who disliked Caesar intensely, while plunged into gloom by his military success, was not so sure that Pompey was really very much the better of the two. And he confided as much privately to his friend Atticus:

Absolute power is what both Pompey and Caesar have sought. Their aim has not been to secure the happiness and honour of the community. Pompey has not abandoned Rome because it was impossible to defend, nor Italy under forced compulsion. But it was his idea from the first to plunge the world into war, to stir up barbarous princes, to bring savage tribes into Italy under arms, and to gather a huge army. A sort of Sulla's reign has long been his object, and is the desire of many of his companions.

Or do you think that no agreement, no compromise between him and Caesar was possible? Why, it *is* possible, today. But neither of them looks to our happiness. Both want to be kings.

(Cicero, *Letters to Atticus*, VIII, 11)

That was what Cicero was thinking and writing on 27 February 49 BC, and within three weeks from that time the 'abandonment of Italy' which he deplored had become the most literal reality. For on 4 March, in order to escape from Caesar's rapidly advancing troops, the two consuls put out across the Adriatic with part of the Pompeian army, and on the 17th Pompey himself, after withdrawing his troops to Brundusium (Brindisi), skilfully extricated himself from the enemy blockade and took to the sea in his turn. Until the last moment Caesar had fervently hoped against hope that he might still be able to detach him from his conservative allies, but all hope of achieving this now had to be abandoned. Indeed, in due course, he would clearly have to follow him across the Adriatic, and invite the decisive clash.

But the time for that had not yet come. First of all, he had to deal with urgent matters at Rome. And, on the way, he insisted on seeing Cicero, whose tongue seemed to be worth a legion or two. The two men met at Formiae (Formia), and Caesar asked the orator to go to Rome and attend the next meeting of the senate, since his absence would look like a hostile gesture towards himself. But Cicero insisted that, if he did go to the meeting, he would feel obliged to speak in support of Pompey and his friends. So his interview with Caesar achieved nothing.

We were mistaken in supposing that he would be easy to deal with – far from it! He told me that my refusal was a vote of censure against him, that all the others would drag their feet if I did not come ... The upshot was, since he apparently wanted to be finished, that 'I was to think it over.' I could not say No, and so we parted.

(Cicero, *Letters to Atticus*, IX, 18)

But before the two men separated, Caesar made it clear that Cicero's assistance was by no means indispensable: if he could not have the benefit of the orator's counsel, then 'he would get advice from wherever he could'. Nevertheless, when he arrived in Rome, he again attempted to secure friendly relations with the former governing class, appealing to the senate to collaborate with him. But the meeting at which he launched the appeal was poorly attended, especially by senior senators, and Caesar concluded by declaring that if they would not help him run the country then he would run it by himself. Next, in spite of a tribune who tried to stop him, he went to the Temple of Saturn, which housed the treasury, and forcibly transferred its contents, which the Pompeian consuls had failed to remove with them, into his own hands. Soon afterwards, he left the capital; and he did so in a very irritated mood because he had received so little cooperation. Cicero, on the other hand, was encouraged by the lukewarm nature of his reception at Rome, and when Pompey summoned every senator to join him at Thessalonica (Salonica) in Macedonia, the orator decided, after prolonged wavering, to respond to the summons, although, when it came to fighting, he did not intend to join in.

But there was to be no fighting in Greek lands at present, for Caesar was not ready to deal with Pompey yet. First of all, he felt he must turn his attention to the west. Grain was urgently needed in Italy, and its provision was menaced by Pompey's superiority at sea. So the grain-producing island of Sicily was seized by Caesar's loyal supporter, Curio, and Sardinia too was brought over. Next, Caesar himself set off by land to attack the great remaining Pompeian stronghold in western Europe, which was Spain. On the

way, he found that Rome's ancient ally Massilia (Marseille), a prosperous Greek city-state, while declaring its neutrality in the struggle between Pompey and Caesar, had belied this pronouncement by admitting Caesar's enemy Ahenobarbus within the gates to organise the city's defences. So Caesar determined to blockade Massilia's port, and for this purpose ordered the construction of ships. Then he passed on to Spain, where six of his legions had been moved from Gaul and awaited his orders. The Pompeian force, though slightly smaller than Caesar's, was formidable all the same, because its commanders, Afranius and Petreius, had learnt from local experience how to operate in a number of small units, which could rapidly be regrouped when the need arose. Moreover, Caesar soon got into difficulties when his bridges were broken by snow-floods, and he found himself cut off on a peninsula. But he escaped from this predicament upon light rafts of a kind that he had seen in Britain; and in the end he cornered the enemy beside a northern tributary of the Ebro, near Ilerda (Lerida). On 27 August the Pompeians, short of water, surrendered, and Caesar, maintaining the clement policy he had recently inaugurated, let Afranius and Petreius go free, and dismissed their soldiers as well, dispensing them from further military service. Meanwhile, Massilia, too, had been compelled to capitulate, and its long career of independence was at an end.

Yet this success won by Caesar was counterblanced by reverses suffered by his subordinates. One of them, Antony's brother, had been defeated by the Pompeian fleet and driven to suicide on an island of the Adriatic. Meanwhile Curio, fresh from his successes in Sicily, had crossed over from that island to north Africa to confront Juba, the king of Numidia (E.Algeria), who possessed powerful cavalry and detested Caesar. But not long after his arrival, Curio was defeated and killed. Moreover, there was serious trouble nearer home. Caesar was still at Massilia, preparing to return to Rome, when he received grim news from north Italy. For a mutiny had broken out among his troops at Placentia (Piacenza). This was a novel experience for him, and one which the *Civil War* disdains to mention, thus revealing that even if this fine work does not usually tell untruths, the narration of the whole truth is likewise not part of its function.

The mutineers belonged to a legion which had suffered severely in Spain, and any chance of increasing their loot, which had been scanty, was annoyingly diminished by Caesar's new policy of

OPPOSITE Reconstruction of Caesar's siege tower and machine at the siege of Massilia (49 BC).

clemency. So he was obliged to hasten to Placentia and deal with their unwelcome and violent complaints. The historian Appian gives a plausible account of the speech he delivered to the disaffected troops, and the outcome of this embarrassing affair.

The mutineers cried out against their officers for prolonging the war and not paying them the bonuses that Caesar had promised them while they were still at Brundusium. When Caesar heard of this, he hastened from Massilia to Placentia and, coming before the soldiers, who were still in a state of mutiny, addressed them as follows:

'You know what kind of speed I use in everything I undertake. This war was not prolonged by us, but by the enemy, who keep retiring from us. You reaped great advantages from my command in Gaul, and you took an oath for me for the whole of this war and not for a part only. And now you abandon us in the midst of our labours, you revolt against your officers, you propose to give orders to those whose orders you are bound to obey. Being myself the witness of my liberality to you heretofore I shall now execute the law of our country by executing every tenth man of the ninth legion, where this mutiny began.'

Straightaway a cry went up from the whole legion, and the officers threw themselves at Caesar's feet in supplication. Caesar yielded little by little and so far remitted the punishment as to designate a hundred and twenty only (who seemed to have been the leaders of the revolt), and he chose twelve of these by lot to be put to death. One of the twelve proved that he was absent when the conspiracy was formed, and Caesar put to death in his place the centurion who had accused him.

(Appian, *Civil Wars*, II, 47)

Probably Caesar had never really intended to inflict such an unpopular and uneconomical punishment as the proposed decimation, but declared his intention to do so in order to give himself an opportunity to display subsequent indulgence. Nor, in all probability, did the lots that decided who was to be put to death fall wholly by accident; the manipulation of the lot was an art with which Roman politicians were all too familiar. As for those of the ringleaders who were spared, they no doubt had their names carefully recorded, so that on battlefields of a later date they could be unobtrusively thrust into dangerous situations.

It had now become imperative for Caesar to return to the capital, and he paid it his second visit of the year. He had by no means abandoned his longstanding ambition to become consul in the following year (48 BC). But a technical obstacle had now presented itself. According to the constitution, elections to consulships had to be conducted by the current consuls: but they were far away with Pompey. There was, however, one way out, and Caesar took it, by securing the passage of a law which invested him with the dictatorship. His initial tenure, at this juncture, of the traditional emergency post of dictator was very brief, but the conferment became, by hindsight, of considerable significance since this was to prove the office on which he eventually decided to depend for his autocratic power. Meanwhile, this first dictatorship was useful since it solved the immediate constitutional problem. For he was now able, by virtue of it, to preside over consular elections in place of the absent consuls: and in this capacity he secured the appointment of himself and a pliant supporter as consuls for the following year.

But he needed the dictatorship for another important purpose as well. For he regarded it as urgently necessary to deal at once with a perilous and far-reaching national problem – the problem of debt. So formidable was this problem, and so determined his attempts to solve it, that these endeavours, on a long-term view, may justly be regarded as one of his greatest positive contributions to the Roman world. Since, however, the measures he felt obliged to take were necessarily somewhat technical and undramatic in appearance, they were not dwelt on at any length by the ancient writers: and since they were unconnected with any contemporary military operation, Caesar does not describe them in his *Civil War*.

At least it is clear, however, that owing to the disturbances of the past half century and more, many Romans and Italians had fallen grievously into debt: and that the harsh laws governing such situations threw these men completely on the untender mercy of money-lenders, and thus cast many of them into utter destitution. Caesar knew all about this sequence of causes and effects not only because he had once been burdened with debts himself, but because, at an earlier stage of his official career, he had tried to deal with the very same problem in Spain. In Rome, too, for several decades past, many other politicians too had been well aware of the deplorable position that had arisen, and most of all at the time of the Catilinarian conspiracy, which owed much of its support to debtors reduced by their predicament to desperation. But would-be reformers were faced by a serious dilemma. On the one hand, something must obviously be done to rescue the ruined debtors. On the other hand, however, the rehabilitation of these unfortunate men must not be allowed to turn into a general cancellation of debts, which would destroy private property, the basis of the entire social system, and thus plunge Rome into a state

121

A battle scene on a later
Roman sarcophagus.

123

of revolution: and that was what even moderate conservatives greatly feared.

During the months that had elapsed since the beginning of the civil war, the debt crisis had become much greater. This was partly because of a shortage of currency. Money had been withdrawn from circulation to be hoarded until times became better, and such cash as could still be found had gone to pay the rival armies. This meant that whereas debtors were now receiving pressing claims for repayment, they were unable to respond to them and had to forfeit their land and other possessions instead, at wretched prices. So Caesar now began a long, patient series of attempts to deal with this harrowing situation. First, the hoarding of coin was forbidden – though such a veto, unsupported by other measures, was not very likely to prove effective. Secondly, creditors, if offered land and other property in repayment of their loans, were compelled to accept them. But in order that they should not be allowed to pay too cheap a price, Caesar also laid it down that the prices should be assessed at the sums the property in question had been worth before the civil war began – these assessments to be made by commissioners specially appointed for the purpose.

Creditors, of course, complained bitterly. But some of them were prepared to admit that they had expected even worse. At least Caesar had not proved the totally revolutionary destroyer of private property that he had been widely feared to be. Indeed, it was reassuring for property owners to note that, even if the senior senators were against him on political grounds, the able financiers were mostly on his side. So confidence began to come back, and men started to lend money once again.

All this had been done by Caesar in the course of only eleven days at Rome. Then, finally, he moved against Pompey in the Balkans. True to his favourite strategy of fighting from careful prepared positions of superior force, Pompey was spending the winter in the mobilisation of the enormous resources of the east. Towards the end of 49 BC (two months earlier by the seasons) he learnt that Caesar had left Rome, and was already at the southern port of Brundusium, hoping to embark and cross the Adriatic. In consequence, Pompey himself moved westwards from Macedonia towards the shores of the Ionian Sea facing Italy, so as to combat an eventual landing. However, he felt no particular sense of urgency, since maritime navigation was normally suspended during the winter months.

On this occasion, however, as on others, he had underestimated Caesar's powers of rapid, improvised action: for whatever nautical tradition might assert, Caesar had every intention of getting over from Italy to Greece. On arrival at Brundusium, he had been deeply disappointed to find that there were not enough ships available to transport his whole army across the sea – if there had been, he later said, the whole war might have been finished in quick time. Nevertheless, on 4 January 48 BC (early November according to the seasons) he succeeded in making the first fateful step. That is to say, taking advantage of a favourable wind, he ferried twenty thousand infantry and six hundred cavalry across, landing on the open shore of Epirus, in what is now Albanian territory. His old enemy Bibulus, who had been his fellow-consul eleven years earlier and now held a naval command on Pompey's side, failed to stop him, but instead, catching thirty of his returning ships, massacred their entire crews; and then died of exhaustion. Meanwhile, the Pompeian land-army, although it did not attempt an engagement, came up very close to the force landed by Caesar, who experienced a nerve-racking delay of three months before Antony was able to bring the main body over to join him. It comprised four legions and eight hundred cavalry.

Nevertheless, time was still not on Caesar's side, since his chances of receiving further reinforcements or supplies by the sea-route were poor. In consequence, he was compelled to take the initiative: and so he struck forcibly at Pompey's key base and storage centre, Dyrrhachium (Durrës, Durazzo). Pompey managed to prevent him just in time by seizing the high ground six miles south of the town. But he could not prevent Caesar from forcing his way between himself and Dyrrhachium. Its fortifications were fourteen miles in circumference, and Caesar built a seventeen-mile entrenchment around them – an astonishing achievement for an army out-numbered by five to four. However, Caesar's six-pronged attack on the fortress failed, and shortly afterwards Pompey punctured the southern extremity of his lines. Caesar's counter-attack failed disastrously, costing the lives of more than a thousand of his legionaries, whom he could ill afford to lose. If Pompey had followed up his victory, it was said (by Caesar himself among others) that he might have won the entire war on that single day. But he took no such action; amid the maze of entrenchments, he probably did not realize how big a success he had won.

For Caesar's attempted blockade had been completely smashed. He recoiled hastily into the interior of Thessaly; and the forces of

Reconstruction of Caesar's confrontation with Pompey outside Dyrrhachium (Durazzo, Durrës), 48 BC.

Pompey followed him. Before long, the two armies were facing each other, in scorching weather, upon the plain of Pharsalus. Although Caesar was now outnumbered by two to one, and his enemies were stationed on higher ground, he could not delay, and repeatedly offered battle. But in vain. Finally, he decided, in despair, that he would soon have to break away altogether, and seek a new theatre of war in a different region. But at this moment he saw, to his profound satisfaction, that Pompey was preparing to fight after all. There were dissensions among his fellow leaders, and Labienus had persuaded him to take an over-sanguine view of the decline of the other side's morale. So the plan of avoiding battle was discarded by the Pompeians, and they decided to engage. And now it was Labienus, once again, who induced Pompey to adopt a plan whereby legionary blood would be saved; the victory was to be won not so much by the legions as by foreign auxiliaries, namely his seven thousand cavalry, who at a

126

carefully timed moment during the engagement would deliver a flank attack against Caesar's right wing. Caesar, however, who knew the workings of Labienus' mind, anticipated this move, and, instead of fighting in the usual formation of three lines, planned to retain a fourth line out of sight, drawn up at an angle in support of the threatened wing – of which he himself assumed command. But this move, and the course of the battle which now followed – the largest ever to be fought between Romans – can be seen through the eyes of Caesar himself.

Fearing that his right wing might be surrounded by the large numbers of the Pompeian cavalry, he quickly took one cohort from each legion from his third line and formed them into a fourth line, which he stationed opposite the cavalry. He gave them their instructions, and warned them that that day's victory would depend on the valour of those cohorts. He also ordered the third line and the army as a whole not to charge without his command, saying that he would give a signal with his flag when he wished them to do so.

In giving the usual address of encouragement to the troops, in which he related the good service they had done him at all times, he recalled above all that he could call the troops to witness the earnestness with which he had sought peace ... It had never been his wish to expose his troops to bloodshed, nor to deprive the State of either army. After this speech, at the insistence of his troops, who were afire with enthusiasm, he gave the signal by trumpet ...

Between the two armies there was just enough space left for them to advance and engage each other. Pompey, however, had told his men to wait for Caesar's onset, and not to move from their positions or allow the line to be split up. He was said to have done this on the advice of Gaius Triarius, with the intention of breaking the force of the first impact of the enemy and stretching out their line, so that his own men, who were still in formation, could attack them while they were scattered. He also thought that the falling javelins would do less damage if the men stood still than if they were running forward while the missiles were discharged. More-over, Caesar's troops, having to run twice the distance, would be out of breath and exhausted. It appears to us that he did this without sound reason, for there is a certain eagerness of spirit and an innate keenness in everyone which is inflamed by desire for battle. Generals ought to encourage this, not repress it; nor was it for nothing that the practice began in antiquity of giving the signal on both sides and everyone's raising a war-cry; this was believed both to frighten the enemy and to stimulate one's own men.

Our men, on the signal, ran forward with javelins levelled; but when they observed that Pompey's men were not running to meet them, thanks to the practical experience and training they had had in earlier battles, they checked their charge and halted about half-way, so as not to approach worn out. Then after a short interval they renewed the charge, threw their javelins and, as ordered by Caesar, quickly drew their swords. Nor indeed did the Pompeians fail to meet the occasion. They stood up to the hail of missiles and bore the onset of the legions; they kept their ranks, threw their javelins, and then resorted to their swords. At the same time the cavalry all charged forward, as instructed, from Pompey's left wing, and the whole horde of archers rushed out. Our cavalry failed to withstand their onslaught; they were dislodged from their position and gave ground a little. Pompey's cavalry thereupon pressed the more hotly and began to deploy in squadrons and surround our line on its exposed flank. Observing this, Caesar gave the signal to the fourth line which he had formed of single cohorts. They ran forward swiftly to the attack with their standards and charged at Pompey's cavalry with such force that none of them could hold ground. They all turned, and not only gave ground but fled precipitately to the hilltops. Their withdrawal left all the archers and slingers exposed, and, unarmed and unprotected, they were killed. In the same charge the cohorts surrounded the Pompeians who were still fighting and putting up a resistance on the left wing, and attacked them in the rear.

At the same time Caesar gave the order to advance to the third line, which had done nothing and had stayed in its position up till then. As a result, when fresh and unscathed troops took the place of the weary, while others were attacking from the rear, the Pompeians could not hold out, and every one of them turned tail and fled.

(Caesar, *Civil War*, III, 89–94)

After watching the disaster, Pompey rode straight back to his camp, but the victorious Caesarians, in spite of the great heat, came closely behind and began to storm the camp – just as Pompey himself departed in haste by the rear gate, and rode away towards the Aegean coast. As he went, he complained constantly that it was his cavalry that had let him down.

Whatever the causes, the result had been overwhelming defeat: fifteen thousand of Pompey's men were killed, and more than twenty-four thousand surrendered. True – except for Ahenobarbus, who was among the fallen – most of the leading Pompeians escaped to fight Caesar again another day. But for Pompey it was the end. Now he could never be the ruler of the Roman world, and henceforward the mastery lay with Caesar.

When he arrived at the camp shortly after his defeated enemy had vacated it, he ate the dinner that had been prepared for Pompey, and did not fail to point out the unsuitable luxuriousness of the tents of the Republican leaders. Nevertheless, in order to avoid a reign of terror among Roman noblemen, he burnt the correspondence of Pompey and Metellus unread. Soon afterwards, he went on for a tour of the battlefield, and made two widely publicised utterances. One of them was a reminder that, had he not called upon his army for assistance, all his services to his country would not have availed to save him, once he had reverted to private status, from prosecution and condemnation in the courts. Next, Caesar gazed upon the many corpses, and declared: *It was all their own doing.'*

Then he crossed over to Asia Minor, and compelled its rich cities to part with the funds he needed to give his soldiers the rewards they demanded and deserved – and the money might also be needed to pursue the struggle against Pompey's sons and followers, if, as was not certain at the present, they decided to continue the fight.

6
Caesar and Cleopatra in Egypt

MEANWHILE POMPEY, TOO, HAD SAILED, and landed briefly at various Aegean harbours. But his reception at these ports was discouraging, and he decided to go on to Egypt. In 51 BC, Ptolemy XII the Piper, the king of this nominally independent country, had died, and was jointly succeeded by his son Ptolemy XIII, aged ten, and his daughter Cleopatra VII (the boy's half sister), who was eighteen and a half. The courts of the two new monarchs were separate and profoundly hostile to one another, and, in the course of a rapid series of attempted coups and counter-coups, Cleopatra succeeded for a time in seizing sole power for herself. However, since she enjoyed the support of hardly any of the national leaders, who feared she would be much less malleable than her very youthful half-brother, she was very soon expelled by his Regency Council, and fled across the limits of Egypt to take refuge in the Judaean borderland in 48 BC. Against her, upon the lower slopes of Mount Casius (Ras Baron) some thirty miles beyond the frontier, was the army of the boy king Ptolemy XIII. His Regency Council had come to the assistance of Pompey in the Roman civil war, and, in recognition of this aid, Pompey's émigré senate at Thessalonica (Salonica) had decreed that he should be appointed the young king's guardian. After the disaster at Pharsalus, Pompey remembered this good excuse for intervention in the country; and he also hoped that his entertainment of the boy's late father in Italy gave him a further claim upon Egyptian hospitality. Bearing these points in mind, he now decided that, even though Egypt was not Roman territory, it provided the most promising site for a headquarters from which he could direct developments in the various parts of the empire, such as north Africa and Spain, in which his following was still strong. But when he landed beneath the slopes of Mount Casius, the king's Greco-Egyptian general Achillas, accompanied by two renegade Roman officers, went out in a boat to meet him, and he was struck down and murdered.

They wanted to be on the winning side. And they also wanted to give Caesar no excuse whatever for staying on Egyptian soil. For he was known to be on the way, in hot pursuit of Pompey. And indeed, only four days after Pompey's death, he arrived in Alexandria harbour, with ten warships from the allied city-state of Rhodes, and a small force of 3,200 infantry and 800 cavalry. On his arrival, he was promptly shown Pompey's severed head. But any hope that he might now decide to move on elsewhere proved entirely illusory.

PREVIOUS PAGES The Nile.

132

This was because he first intended to exhort an enormous sum of money from this wealthy country. For this demand, he maintained, there was the fullest possible justification. When he had been consul in 59 BC, he and Pompey had agreed to confirm Ptolemy the Piper's title to the throne in exchange for huge gifts of money, which Ptolemy had raised by borrowing from the Roman financier Gaius Rabirius Postumus. When Postumus claimed (no doubt falsely) that his efforts to persuade Ptolemy to repay were unsuccessful, Caesar had personally assumed the responsibility of getting his money back for him – thus providing himself with an excellent excuse for interference when a suitable opportunity arose. That time had now come.

On the death of the Piper, Caesar had taken the opportunity to remind the new monarchs of their debt, which still, he pointed out, remained unpaid. But at the same time he had offered a gracious gesture, by reducing their indebtedness to only half of the total sum that was alleged to be outstanding. This sum he had now come to collect, since, like the sums recently exhorted in Asia Minor, it was needed to pay his soldiers and prepare, if necessary, for further operations against the late Pompey's followers. He was also in a position to comment unpleasantly on the help Egypt had given Pompey in order to fight against himself. However, the *Civil War* does not choose to dwell upon this point, but prefers, with a certain disingenuousness, to give quite other reasons for Caesar's refusal to fall in with the Egyptians' obvious desire that he should quit their country at the earliest possible moment.

He was unable to move because of the prevailing northwest winds which at this time make it impossible to get out of Alexandria. Meanwhile he came to the conclusion that the quarrel between the two rulers of Egypt affected the Roman people and consequently himself as consul. Indeed he was himself particularly closely concerned with Egypt since it was during his previous consulship that the alliance had been made between Rome and the elder Ptolemy [XII] – an alliance ratified both by law and by a decree of the Roman senate. Caesar therefore made it known that he wished King Ptolemy [XIII] and his sister Cleopatra to disband their armies, to appear before him, and to settle their dispute in a legal way rather than by force of arms.

(Caesar, *Civil War*, III, 107)

Since this high-minded task of arbitration was going to be his official pretext for intervention, he decided that, in spite of Egypt's status as a foreign country, it was appropriate that he should land in the guise of a Roman consul, escorted by the

133

OPPOSITE Detail of *The Siege of Alesia*, by Melchior Feselen (1495–1538).

LEFT Caesar's enemy Ahenobarbus, who surrendered to him at Corfinium.
BOTTOM Characteristic art of Caesar's epoch: mosaic at Praeneste (Palestrina), showing a Nile scene.

customary twelve lictors carrying the bundles of rods that symbol-ised his office. However, this method of entering the country caused a hostile and violent demonstration from the Alexandrian populace and troops, who bitterly resented this infringement of Egyptian sovereignty, and continued to riot for several days, during which a number of Caesar's legionaries were murdered. Nevertheless, he moved into the palace, and sent word to Ptolemy XIII, who was still with his army on the frontier, to report to him in Alexandria. Some two weeks later the boy arrived, but his chief minister, the eunuch Pothinus, who was determined to protect his nation's independence, displayed a deliberately uncooperative attitude, suggesting that there were surely other countries altogether in which Caesar's presence was more pressingly needed and desired. Pothinus also arranged that his royal master's dinner table should display nothing but utterly decrepit-looking dishes made of earthenware and wood, which made it possible to insinuate that all the expensive plate had been taken by Caesar. Furthermore, Pothinus ensured that only the nastiest sort of grain should be delivered to the Roman soldiers for their food, since, not being entitled to Egyptian supplies, they were very fortunate, he declared, to be given anything to eat at all.

Within a few weeks, Cleopatra followed her half-brother's example, and responded to Caesar's summons. Indeed, it is very likely that she would have tried to come to him even if he had not summoned her at all. She had, it is true, already sent him a letter stating her claims to the throne. Yet she felt sure, as the historian Dio Cassius duly noted, that her arguments were more likely to prove effective if she could find an opportunity to exploit her personal charms. Her journey was by no means lacking in peril, since her access to Alexandria both by land and by sea was barred by the forces of Ptolemy, under the direction of Pothinus. Nevertheless, she managed to overcome these difficulties; and Plutarch's *Life of Caesar*, telling a story repeated by countless authors and film-producers of later times, explains how she did it.

Taking only one of her friends with her, namely Apollodorus the Sicilian, she embarked in a small boat and landed at the palace when it was already growing dark. Since there seemed to be no other way of getting in unobserved, she stretched herself out at full length inside a sleeping bag, and Apollodorus, after tying up the bag, carried it indoors to Caesar. This little trick of Cleopatra's, which showed her provocative impudence, is said to have been the first thing about her which captivated Caesar ...

(Plutarch, *Caesar*, 49)

As all the world knows, the process of captivation was very rapidly completed; and in next to no time the fifty-two-year-old consul, and the queen thirty-one years younger than himself, had embarked on a love-affair in the royal palace.

For the personal appearance of Cleopatra we have to depend on her coin portraits, which do not greatly fire the imagination; for no identifiable portrait-bust survives. But we also have a brief, evocative comment by Plutarch, which Sir Thomas North, whose version inspired Shakespeare, rendered as follows:

Her beauty, as it is reported, was not so passing as to be unmatchable of other women, nor yet such as upon present view did enamour men with her; but so sweet was her company and conversation that a man could not possibly but be taken. And, besides her beauty, the good grace she had to talk and discourse, her courteous nature that tempered her words and deeds, was a spur that pricked to the quick. Furthermore, besides all these, her voice and words were marvellous pleasant; for her tongue was an instrument of music to divers sports and pastimes, the which she easily turned to any language that pleased her.

(Plutarch, Antony, 27)

But Plutarch's reference to Cleopatra's 'provocative impudence', quoted above, is in danger of creating a misapprehension, since although perfectly prepared to employ any such wiles to ensnare Ceasar, she was very different from the uninformed, kittenish, adolescent of Bernard Shaw's *Caesar and Cleopatra*. On the contrary, she was a young woman of formidable brain-power and overwhelming, ruthless ambition for herself and her country. Her supreme desire was to see Egypt, with herself at its head, reviving the great, powerful empire it had possessed two and a half centuries previously, under the earliest Ptolemies. But how was this to be done? Men such as Pothinus, who were as patriotic as she was, believed that it could only be achieved by rigorous opposition to the encroachments planned by Caesar. Cleopatra took the opposite view. She had loved her father and shared his vicissitudes and humiliations, and as a result she had concluded that his policy, which was to be on good terms with Rome, was entirely right – since there was no possible alternative. She had to use the Romans, and that meant, at this juncture, that she had to win the favour of Caesar. Since he was the most brilliant man of his epoch this was presumably no great hardship, provided she did not find their disparity in age too unattractive.

Caesar had come to Egypt to finish off Pompey; and he had stayed on to raise money. This money, presumably, had still not

Caesar at the Tomb of Alexander the Great in Alexandria, by Sébastien Bourdon (1616–71).

139

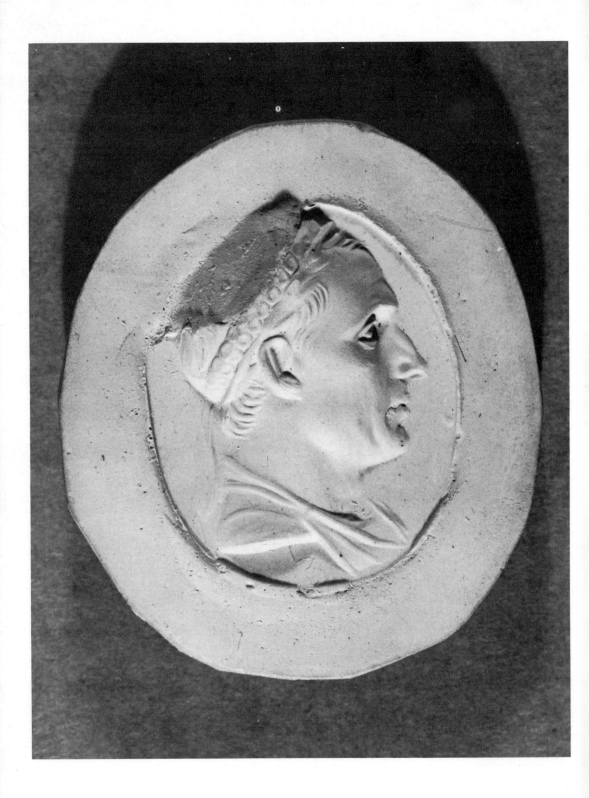

come his way, but in any case there were now two further reasons
why he stayed on. For one thing, the local political situation was
disturbed and threatening, and needed his attention. And, besides,
he evidently found Cleopatra a fascinating mistress. Which motive
weighed the heavier with him, we cannot say. To suggest that if
Egypt had not turned against him, and if he had at once got his
hands on the funds he wanted, he would have left straightaway,
regardless of Cleopatra, sounds depressingly unromantic. However, that is what he might have done. But it is equally possible
that he would have done no such thing, since his interest in
women as sexual objects, and no doubt as companions as well, was
enormous. In early life, as his enemies were never tired of recalling,
he may have passed through a homosexual phase. But if so, he had
got over this quickly, and became not only a much-married man,
but an indefatigable womaniser. To believe all recorded ancient
gossip would be a mistake, but when the various writers are so
unanimous on this particular point the conclusion that there is no
smoke without fire remains legitimate, and indeed unavoidable.
So he must have been very susceptible to Cleopatra's charms: and
they duly had their effect, in no uncertain fashion.

So the thirteen-year-old Ptolemy XIII, holding his court in the
same royal palace, suffered two terrible shocks in rapid succession;
first, the arrival of Cleopatra, who was supposed to be outside the
country, and then her immediate establishment in Caesar's bed.
Pothinus prompted the young king to whip up a demonstration
against the lovers among the Alexandrian populace, and the

OPPOSITE Chalcedony
intaglio of Julius Caesar,
made in Egypt at the time
when he was celebrating his
victory in the Alexandrian war

141

dangerous incidents that ensued impelled Caesar to work seriously at his self-imposed task of bringing the royal half-brother and half-sister together into renewed fraternal love. His efforts proved outwardly successful, and the ostensible reconciliation between the two monarchs that followed was celebrated by lavish thanksgivings. Indeed it was probably now, in accordance with Egyptian custom, that they went through a formal ceremony of marriage, which remained unconsummated.

At the same time Caesar sought to ingratiate himself with the Egyptians by returning the Roman province of Cyprus, a former Ptolemaic possession, to the Ptolemaic house, in the persons of the princess Arsinoe IV, who was a girl of between seventeen and twenty, and Ptolemy XIV, who was eleven. They were respectively sister and brother, and half sister and half brother, to the rulers of Egypt, Ptolemy XIII and Cleopatra who were now officially reconciled.

However, it very soon became clear that the much proclaimed new friendship was entirely hollow. For before the end of October Caesar discovered that Pothinus, presumably with the complicity of the young king, had secretly instructed the royal army on the eastern frontier to march on Alexandria, under the command of Achillas, the officer who had superintended Pompey's murder. Some two weeks later, Caesar learnt that Achillas was approaching the capital with a powerful force, consisting largely of a Roman 'foreign legion' left behind by the triumvirs' henchman Gabinius in the previous decade, after he had forcibly restored the present monarchs' father to the throne of his unwilling country. Caesar, although he deplored the murky background of these warriors of fortune, did not under-estimate the peril they presented.

Achillas had an army which in numbers, quality and military experience was very far from being contemptible. There were twenty thousand men under arms, most of whom had once served under Gabinius, but had now grown accustomed to Alexandrian life with all its licence. They had forgotten what was meant by discipline and by the name of Rome; and had married native wives, by whom many of them had children.

Their numbers were augmented by men gathered together from the bands of pirates and robbers from Syria, the province of Cilicia, and neighbouring parts. They had also been joined by a number of convicts and exiles. Moreover, Alexandria offered a perfectly safe way of escape to our own slaves: all they had to do was to give in their names and join the Egyptian army.

(Caesar, *Civil War*, III, 110)

142

Outnumbered five to one, Caesar appealed to his representatives in Syria and Asia Minor for the urgent dispatch of reinforcements. He also sent two eminent Egyptian envoys to negotiate with Achillas who had them beaten up, and one was killed. Then Achillas marched onwards to Alexandria, and entered the city. Caesar, in the company of Ptolemy XIII (who had been placed under house arrest) and Cleopatra, now found himself barricaded inside the royal palace and unable to get out. His situation was precarious, as an immediate attack on his land-fortifications by Achillas forcibly confirmed. But from the sea, which came right up to the palace enclosure, the threat to his safety was even graver, for Achillas had now brought seventy-two ships, twice the number of the Roman fleet, right inside the adjacent Great Harbour. Caesar, by a master-stroke, succeeded in capturing these vessels, and since they could not be manned they were burnt. The flames spread to the quays and destroyed a large consignment of books that was standing on them – an incident which gave rise to the damaging legend that Caesar had destroyed the great Alexandrian library itself, the greatest library in the world. On the very same day on which he had captured the ships, Caesar also managed to take possession of the world-famous lighthouse, the Pharos, which stood at the western end of the harbour entrance.

But these maritime successes were largely offset by unfortunate political developments within the city itself. Among the members

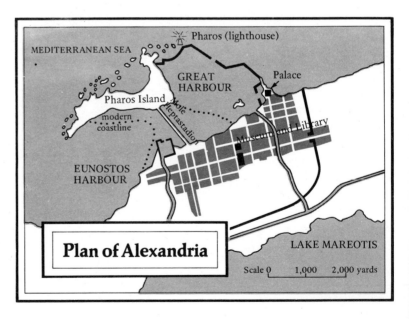

Plan of Alexandria

144

of the royal family confined in the royal palace was Cleopatra's half-sister Arsinoe IV, whom Caesar had not permitted to leave and occupy her kingdom of Cyprus. At this junction, Arsinoe, who hated Cleopatra and her pro-Roman behaviour, managed to slip away from the palace to Achillas, who hailed her as the new queen of Egypt, with enthusiastic support from the Alexandrian populace. However, her principal adviser, the eunuch Ganymedes, was unable to get on friendly terms with Achillas. Ptolemy's chief minister Pothinus, who was watching this situation closely from the beleaguered palace, sent secret messengers to Achillas assuring him of his support. However, the messengers were betrayed to Caesar by Pothinus' barber, and Caesar placed Pothinus under arrest and put him to death. Achillas, too, was now murdered, at the instigation of Ganymedes. But this did not lead to any lull in hostilities, for Ganymedes took over the dead man's command and continued the fight against Caesar with great vigour both on land and at sea. He also tried to pollute the Roman army's water supply by pumping sea-water into their wells. But the legionaries dug all through the night to sink new ones.

Two days later, off the coast not far from Alexandria, a very welcome naval contingent made its appearance: and it was bringing a Roman legion from Asia Minor. Greatly encouraged, Caesar now attacked the long Pharos island adjoining the light-house, and succeeded in overrunning it. But when he went on to assault the mole (Heptastadion) which linked it to the mainland, he suffered a sharp and serious setback. For Egyptian soldiers landed on the mole in the rear of his troops, who thereupon made a mad rush for their warships in any and every small boat they could find; while others dived into the sea. Caesar, for fear of being totally cut off, was compelled to seek refuge on his flagship, which was near at hand. But so many of his men clambered onto its decks with him that the flagship could not be pushed off from the shore. Caesar himself jumped overboard and swam away towards the ships standing further out. He was encumbered by his armour, but his departure was so hasty that he left his purple cloak behind as a trophy for the Egyptians. For, according to Plutarch, he only just managed to get away. He was holding a number of papers in his hand and would not let them go, though he was being shot at from all sides and was often under water. Yet he swam onwards until he was picked up by one of the other vessels.

Meanwhile the flagship from which he had just escaped had sunk, and everyone on board was drowned. Many other soldiers

145

and marines, too, were in difficulties, either struggling in the water or hard-pressed by the Egyptians on land. Caesar now gave orders that small boats should be sent back to them, and a good many men were rescued in this way. Nevertheless, four hundred legionaries had lost their lives, and over two hundred marines and sailors as well.

To distract attention from this defeat, Caesar now took the surprising step of setting Ptolemy XIII free to go wherever he wanted. At the same time he positively encouraged the young king to make his way to the royal army and take over its command, thus superseding Arsinoe's general Ganymedes. Caesar's intention was to provoke friction between the two courts, and perhaps to get rid of the efficient Ganymedes. If so, the plan was partially successful, since from now onwards Ganymedes faded from view. But Ptolemy became Cacsar's open enemy, and the war went on.

However, early in March 47 BC, the relieving army, summoned by Caesar, began to approach Egypt's eastern frontier. The commander of the force was a certain Mithridates of Pergamum, half Greek and half Iranian, and his men were Asians, Syrians and Arabians. As they came near the little principality of Judaea, they were joined by a Jewish contingent, led by the high priest Hyrcanus and his much more forceful chief minister Antipater (the father of Herod the Great). At the beginning of the civil war, they had been obliged to side with Pompey (although the Jews hated him for having entered the Holy of Holies of their Temple at Jerusalem); and now they were eager to rectify this mistake and gain the favour of Caesar instead. During the week-long desert journey across the borderlands of Egypt, Antipater kept Mithridates' army supplied with food and drink. Next, after the frontier fortress Pelusium had been forced to surrender, the presence of the high priest won over the very numerous Egyptian Jews to Caesar's cause.

After marching round the apex of the Nile delta, Mithridates then wheeled northwards towards Alexandria. As he approached the city, he found himself confronted by Ptolemy's much more extensive force. But meanwhile Caesar himself, after deceiving the enemy about his intentions, had managed to slip out of Alexandria by sea, and join up with Mithridates. In the battle that followed the Egyptians were utterly routed. The Gabinian foreign legion which formed the nucleus of their army was virtually wiped out, and Ptolemy, his Nile boat overloaded with fugitives, fell into the river and was drowned. Later, the Romans rescued his body and placed his golden armour on display in Alexandria. After his victory, Caesar made a triumphant re-entry into the city, and the whole population, who had so recently been his fierce enemies, came to greet him as suppliants, carrying all their sacred objects. Then, passing through the barricades which he had so recently needed to protect his life, he returned to the palace once again.

All Egypt was now in his power. Yet he decided that the country should not be annexed and made a Roman province. Its riches would have been too much of a temptation for any governor, and, besides, he owed it to Cleopatra to leave her on the throne. Since, however, convention required that a queen should have a male colleague, he made her surviving half-brother, the twelve-year-old Ptolemy XIV, her joint monarch. Cyprus was added to their kingdom, and Arsinoe transported to Rome to be saved up for Caesar's future Triumph. The Jews, for their contribution to the relief force, were rewarded with various privileges – though these cannot have been welcomed by the Greeks and half-Greeks of Egypt's ruling class, who were markedly anti-Semitic.

In order to cope with possible disturbances from this or other causes, Caesar decided that three Roman legions should stay in the country to support Cleopatra. It was customary for the command of Roman legions and armies, wherever they might be situated, to be conferred upon senators and no one else. But Caesar did not trust any senator with the power and wealth that a legionary force in Egypt could command. Instead of a senator, therefore, the officer to whom Caesar entrusted the legions was a man who had been his own slave, named Rufio. It was his duty to ensure that Cleopatra should not be toppled off her throne – and that neither she nor her eventual successors should become too independent of Rome.

Early in the year 47 BC, Caesar went with Cleopatra for a journey up the Nile. It was played down by later Roman writers because Augustus, whose direct or indirect pressure influenced historiography, deplored Caesar's association with Cleopatra and wanted as little said about it as possible. To fill this vacuum, the trip was subsequently invested with a great deal of prurient romance – so that its practical significance was lost sight of. A few sentences about the cruise, from men writing nearly two centuries later, are all that surviving literary authorities can provide. 'He went up the Nile with four hundred ships, exploring the country in company with Cleopatra and generally enjoying himself with her' (Appian).

'He would have gone through Egypt with her in her state-barge
almost to Ethiopia, had not his soldiers refused to follow him'
(Suetonius). It is probable enough that the expedition comprised a
large number of ships and troops, since both Caesar and Cleopatra
still had numerous Egyptian enemies. And it is not surprising, too,
that the Roman soldiers became restless, because the war was
already won – and they lacked Caesar's personal reasons for
taking pleasure in the excursion. Yet Caesar's motive was not only
the enjoyment of Cleopatra's company, but high politics. It was
necessary to show the flag; steps had to be taken, throughout the
length and breadth of the country, to gain support for the new
regime, and stamp out the opposition to himself and Cleopatra;
for it was not by any means wholly crushed.

Besides, Caesar's enjoyment of the cruise must have been
somewhat modified by Cleopatra's condition. For she was at this
time in approximately her sixth month of pregnancy. And in due
season, probably during the early days of September, she gave
birth to a son. She named him Caesarion after Caesar, and asserted
that Caesar was his father. From that time onwards – and no doubt
already from the time when her pregnancy was first apparent –
this question of Caesarion's paternity was disputed. On balance it
seems likely that Caesar was the father, since at the time of the
infant's conception Caesar and Cleopatra were together in the
palace. Despite her enemies' accusations of promiscuity, Cleopatra
is not known to have slept with any other men but Caesar and,
after Caesar's death, Antony: like other Ptolemaic queens, she was

149

Mosaic from Pompeii, first century BC: Nilotic scenes such as this one may have been made fashionable by Cleopatra's court.

much too proud of her family and of herself to behave promiscuously. Caesar had previously been the father of one child only, a daughter born thirty-six years previously, and now dead. If Caesarion was his child, he was the only son he ever had.

However, he did not stay on in Egypt to await his birth. For in June he said goodbye to Cleopatra – for a short time, and not for ever as Bernard Shaw implied.

Then he departed for Syria, with Asia Minor as his further destination. In both these countries there were urgent matters to be attended to – and, as usual, funds to be raised. Caesar has been criticised for not returning at once to Rome, where he had been elected dictator for the second time but was completely out of touch with what was going on. It has also seemed surprising that he should have allowed Pompey's sons and their advisers so much time to reorganise their forces in north Africa and Spain. But Caesar may not have known how successful this reorganisation was proving; and while he was still in the east, he judged that he had better take the opportunity to deal with all the eastern questions that he could.

The main outstanding problem was in northern Asia Minor. For thirty-five years, in three successive wars, Rome had battled against the monarch of the Black Sea kingdom of Pontus, Mithridates VI the Great. Finally defeated, Mithridates the Great had

150

fled to the Cimmerian Bosphorus (Crimea), where his son Pharnaces had brought about his death in 63 BC. Later, Pharnaces, seeing the Romans so heavily involved in their own civil wars, had crossed over to Asia Minor, and revived the kingdom of his father. One of Caesar's subordinates, Cnaeus Domitius Calvinus, had suffered a defeat at his hands, and the king ordered a massacre of every Roman within reach.

Mithridates VI of Pontus, Rome's enemy in prolonged wars, was finally defeated by Pompey.

But now Caesar himself moved northwards, and approached Pharnaces at Zela (Zile), where Mithridates the Great had once won a notable victory over the Romans. The Pontic army was installed upon a high hill, and Caesar encamped on an eminence five miles away, separated from his enemy by a narrow valley. To his amazement, he saw the king leading his army to attack him. An unidentifiable officer of Caesar's, who wrote the *Alexandrian War*, describes the scene.

Whatever the reason, Pharnaces began to descend the steep side of the valley. Caesar for some time was amused at his vainglorious display and at the way in which his men were crowded together in a position into which no sane enemy would advance. Meanwhile Pharnaces began to climb up the steep hill opposite at the same speed as he had made the sharp descent, and with his troops in order.

Caesar was startled by this incredible rashness – or self-confidence. He was caught off-guard and unprepared; he was simultaneously calling the troops away from the fortification work, ordering them to arm, deploying the legions and forming the battle lines; and the sudden bustle that this occasioned caused great alarm among our men. While the ranks were still not drawn up and our men were in disorder, royal chariots armed with scythes threw them into confusion; however, large numbers of missiles were launched at the chariots and they were soon over-powered. They were followed by the enemy in battle formation.

The battle-cry was raised and they came to grips. We were greatly helped by the nature of the ground, and greatly also by the kindness of the immortal gods, who participate in all the fortunes of war but particularly where it has proved impossible to conduct the battle by reasoned tactics.

(*Alexandrian War*, 74–5)

The result was inevitable. The royal troops were pushed precipitately down the hill, and most of them were killed or captured. As the legionaries overran Pharnaces' camp, he himself escaped on horseback: but not for long, since soon afterwards he succumbed to a rebellion in the Crimea. Writing about the battle to a friend in Rome, Caesar borrowed a Greek epigram: *I came, I saw, I conquered*. Then he made his way back towards Italy.

151

7 The Dictator at Work

WHEN CAESAR LANDED AT TARENTUM (Taranto) in September, he found trouble awaiting him. For one thing, his earlier legislation to relieve the credit crisis had not gone far enough to please the radicals, who wanted a much better deal for the debtors. Taking advantage of Caesar's absence in Alexandria, two men who owed a great deal of money themselves, the praetor Caelius who was Cicero's friend, and a young tribune, Dolabella, proposed a revolutionary cancellation of all debts. However, Caelius came to a violent end, and Dolabella's proposals were brought to a halt by Antony, Caesar's representative in Italy, who took police measures in which eight hundred people lost their lives.

Caesar, returning to Rome, showed marked displeasure, not only with Dolabella, but with Antony as well. This was partly because both of them had been buying up the properties of political exiles and casualties at cheap rates, or even acquiring them free of charge; and Caesar now compelled them to disgorge the proper prices. Nevertheless, he noted the warning signs that these disturbances had disclosed. For evidently his earlier measures, statesmanlike though they had been, had not gone far enough to abate the hardships suffered by debtors. In consequence, he decided to annul all interest accrued since the beginning of the civil war. He also palliated the hardship that currency hoarding was still causing to debtors by insisting that cash be brought out and invested in Italian land. Moreover, the amounts they already paid in interest were to be deducted from future capital repayments. Interest, in recent years, had risen from four to eight per cent and then to nearly twelve, and Suetonius, in a brief passing reference to the subject, estimated that this particular measure wiped out one quarter of the total indebtedness at a single blow.

While grappling with this crisis, Caesar also had to deal with a mutiny among his legionaries in Italy. There had been a mutiny at Placentia two years earlier, and this second one broke out in Campania. The discontented soldiers were men who had served under him in the east, and now they demanded that they should be rewarded or pensioned off. Driving a praetor-elect, the historian Sallust, out of their camp, they set off towards Rome, where they camped upon the Field of Mars, outside the walls. But Caesar suddenly appeared in their midst, and began to speak to them. By the way they had behaved, he declared, they had disqualified themselves from their share of the loot which would have come their way when he eventually celebrated his Triumph. That dashed their spirits; and so did the way in which he spoke to

them, for he addressed them as 'civilians'.

The mutiny came to an end, and only just in time, because by now the forces of Pompey's sons Cnaeus and Sextus in north Africa and Spain were ready for battle. They were associated with other Roman leaders, including Labienus, Afranius, Petreius, and Metellus Scipio – whose aristocratic grandeur earned him the supreme command. These Pompeians had allied themselves with Caesar's enemy, Juba, king of Numidia; and the arch-Republican Cato had performed an epic trek from Cyrenaica to rejoin the cause. Their combined army comprised no less than fourteen legions, or the equivalent, and fifteen thousand cavalry. Against them, Caesar initially could only place six legions in the field (two of them newly recruited), and two thousand horse. It was a

Caesar's enemy, King Juba I of Numidia.

campaign as critical for him as any that had gone before. It is described for us in the *African War*, written by an unknown officer – not the same man who wrote about the Alexandrian operations. Although not fully informed about all Caesar's plans, he was a meticulous and straightforward military historian.

Caesar had no intention of waiting for sufficient ships, or food supplies, or water, or the spring campaigning season. As early as 25 December 47 BC (October, according to the seasons), he was already crossing over from Sicily to north Africa, prepared to plunge his army into active operations just as winter was beginning. Some transports carrying additional troops managed to join him before long, but much time and energy had to be spent in trying to find enough for the men to eat, and there were serious disciplinary troubles on both sides. Metellus Scipio, for a time, persisted in a successful strategy of refusing to fight. However, Caesar finally succeeded in forcing him to give battle. This he did by marching on the maritime city of Thapsus (Ras Dimas), which the enemy could not afford to sacrifice owing to the size of its garrison and stores.

The town stood between the sea and a marshy lake, upon an isthmus from one and a half to three miles in width. When Caesar moved onto this narrow strip of land, the Pompeians were delighted, because they believed they had trapped him. They therefore hastened to block the isthmus at either end, with Metellus Scipio to the north beside the city and Caesar's camp, and Juba and Afranius to the south. This meant that the Pompeian forces were divided into two, and that there was no room for their cavalry to manoeuvre. Nevertheless, they felt it was such a triumph to have penned Caesar in that they could now bring him to battle with complete impunity, and win the entire war. But Caesar also was making his dispositions. First he divided his fleet into two flotillas, one of which was to continue the blockade of Thapsus while the other had orders to sail to a point close to Metellus Scipio's adjacent camp and cause confusion in his army. Then, leaving two legions to protect his own camp, he led the rest against Scipio by land. Caesar found his army drawn up in front of his camp, with sixty-four elephants on the wings. In response, he adopted the usual three line deployment of his legionaries, with cavalry and light armed auxiliaries on their flanks and a fourth oblique line (as at Pharsalus) in the rear of each wing, with special instructions to deal with the elephants.

Yet this was a battle which did not go at all according to his plan, and the writer of the *African War* explains why.

As Caesar was making his tour of the army, he observed Metellus Scipio's army in frantic movement around the rampart, running here and there in confusion and sometimes withdrawing inside the gates, sometimes coming out in a disorderly and reckless fashion. A number of other people began to notice the same thing; then all of a sudden there was an outcry from the officers and recalled veterans. They urged Caesar to give the signal without further delay, since the gods were clearly indicating

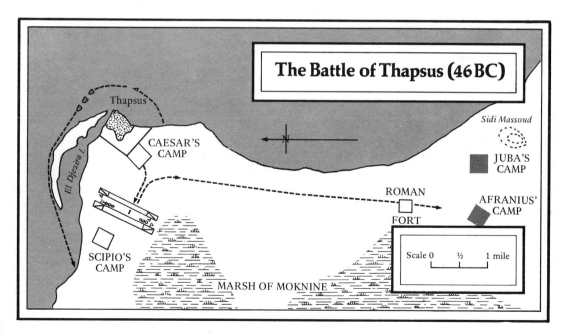

157

An elephant, symbolising Africa, on a coin of Caesar's enemy Metellus Scipio.

that the victory was destined to be theirs. Caesar still hesitated and refused to be budged by their eager insistence. He was bawling out constantly that he did not approve of engaging in battle by an impromptu sally, and repeatedly checking the line from advancing, when suddenly a trumpeter on the right wing, yielding to pressure from the troops and without Caesar's orders, began to sound the call to charge. This was taken up by all the cohorts and they began to advance on the enemy. But the centurions faced about and vainly attempted to restrain their men, urging them not to engage without their commander's orders.

However, Caesar realised that it was impossible to resist his troops' impetuosity. He gave the word 'Good luck' and set his horse at a gallop against the enemy front line. Meanwhile, the slingers and archers on the right wing hurled rapid volleys of missiles at the dense mass of elephants, with the result that the beasts, terrified by the whistling of the sling-shot and the showering stones and lead bullets, turned round and began to trample down their fellows, who were close-packed behind them, and to rush in through the unfinished gateways in the rampart, while the front ranks of the Mauretanian cavalry on the same wing as the elephants also deserted their posts and fled. So our legions quickly got round the elephants and seized the rampart of the enemy; a few of the latter put up a fierce resistance and were killed, but the rest rushed off in flight to the camp they had left the day before.

(*African War*, 82–3)

At the other end of the isthmus, Juba and Afranius heard the disastrous news, and fled as well. The fighting was now virtually over. But it ended in an uglier way than any previous campaign, because Caesar's veterans massacred Scipio's troops, and even killed and wounded a number of senators and knights on their own side, whose loyalty had inspired them with doubts. The supreme Republican, Cato, committed suicide with imposing, philosophical serenity, at the ancient city of Utica (Porto Farina), thus creating a legend which was to prove highly inconvenient to his arch-enemy Caesar. Metellus Scipio, Afranius, and Petreius also met their deaths, their long record of resistance all in vain, and king Juba perished as well. This Numidian kingdom, immensely rich in grain and oil and potential soldiers, was annexed by Rome to become the province of New Africa (Africa Nova), with Sallust as its first governor. Yet, even if the African campaign was concluded, the civil war was still not by any means over. For the two sons of Pompey and Labienus managed to make their escape once again, to fight on yet another day.

But Caesar did not feel free to deal with them yet. Before the end of July 46 BC, he was back in the capital. It became incumbent upon Cicero, spared by Caesar and, despite all the hostility in his heart, outwardly courteous, to address him pleas of mercy for two of his defeated enemies. In his speech for Marcus Claudius Marcellus, Caesar's enemy who was now living in banishment, Cicero skilfully mingles compliments with a firm but tactful request to restore the Republic – a request, as it seemed to the orator, which it was imperative to address to the man who had just been elected dictator for the third time, on this occasion for the unprecedented duration of ten years. Cicero's pretext came because Caesar held the view of the Epicurean philosophers that there was nothing frightening about the prospect of death.

> Of all the wonders that I yet have heard,
> It seems to me most strange that men should fear;
> Seeing that death, a necessary end,
> Will come when it will come.

(Shakespeare, Julius Caesar, II, 2)

This philosophical opinion had now become of general concern, because Caesar (although he was only fifty-four) was believed to have remarked that he had already lived quite long enough. This was unacceptable, said Cicero, because the war wounds still had to be healed; and the only man who could heal them was Caesar.

If, then, Gaius Caesar, the outcome of your mortal deeds is that, after crushing your enemies, you propose to take your leave of the common-wealth while it is still in the condition in which it finds itself today, you will run the risk, for all your superhuman exploits, of gaining astonishment rather than glory as your reward: if, that is to say, we are right to interpret glory as meaning a brilliant universal renown earned by mighty services to one's fellow citizens and one's country and the world.

This phase, then, still awaits you. This act of the drama has not yet been played. This is the programme to which you must devote all your energies: the re-establishment of the constitution, with yourself the first to reap its fruits in profound tranquillity and peace.

(Cicero, *On Behalf of Marcellus*, VIII, 26 – IX, 27)

Marcellus was duly pardoned, though he did not live to return to Rome. Shortly afterwards, Cicero spoke in favour of another man deep in Caesar's disfavour, Quintus Ligarius, who had continued to fight against him at Thapsus and had been forbidden to return to Italy. Plutarch gives an account of Caesar's reaction to the speech.

When Cicero began to speak, his words were incredibly moving; and as his speech proceeded, ranging in the most wonderfully charming language from one emotion to another, the colour came and went on Caesar's face and it was evident that every passion of his soul was being stirred. And finally, when the orator touched on the battle at Pharsalus, Caesar was so deeply affected that his whole body shook and the papers that he was holding dropped from his hand. So he was overpowered, and acquitted Ligarius.

(Plutarch, *Cicero*, 39)

Of the restoration of the Republic, however, there was no sign at all.

Instead, all attention was concentrated on Caesar's personal achievement. For during the last ten days of September 46 BC Caesar celebrated four magnificent, gigantically expensive Triumphs, forming spectacles which in later ages kindled the imagination of Mantegna and many another painter. Since it would not have been proper to commemorate victories over fellow-Romans, each of the Triumphs was named after a defeated foreign country – Gaul, Egypt, Pontus and Africa. The numbers of enemies killed (excluding the fallen Roman citizens) were estimated, no doubt with exaggeration, at 1,192,000. There were also notable prisoners to be seen: Vercingetorix, who was executed after the display; king Juba's four-year-old son, who lived to become a king himself, under Roman protection; and Cleopatra's half-sister, Arsinoe. She, too, was spared, but meanwhile her appearance at the Triumph had earned compassion among the Romans, and the display of pictures gloatingly portraying the

162

deaths of leading Romans – Cato, Metellus Scipio and Petreius – likewise elicited their disapproval.

Certain other awkward incidents also occurred. For example, the axle of Caesar's chariot broke in two; and in deference to superstition he felt it prudent to climb up the steps of the Capitol on his knees, to ward off the omen. His soldiers too did not always behave in a welcome fashion. It was customary for the troops, on these occasions, to sing satirical songs about their generals; and they revived this custom now. When they referred to Caesar's autocratic ambitions, he avoided showing displeasure. But at his Gallic triumph, they also sang a song referring to his reputation as a chaser of women.

> Home we bring our bald whoremonger:
> Romans, lock your wives away!
> All the bags of gold you lent him
> Went his Gallic tarts to pay.

How Caesar reacted to these crude verses we do not know. But it was a different matter when the legionaries also ranged back further into the past, and revived the story that Caesar, thirty years previously, had been the homosexual associate of king Nicomedes of Bithynia:

> Gaul was brought to shame by Caesar;
> By king Nicomedes, he.
> Here comes Caesar, wreathed in triumph
> For his Gallic victory!
> Nicomedes wears no laurels,
> Though the greatest of the three.

This ancient gossip profoundly irritated Caesar, who at once denied with great emphasis that he had ever been involved in any such relationship with Nicomedes. Caesar was also annoyed with a sixty-year-old knight and popular playwright, Decimus Laberius, who, feeling humiliated because he had been compelled to act in one of his own plays, inserted lines referring to the loss of freedom, and dwelling upon the fear in which the man who inspires fear must inevitably live. These unfortunate allusions occurred during the course of the lavish entertainments which accompanied the Triumphs. Indeed, the entertainments were much too lavish altogether, according to some of the soldiers, who complained that they would have preferred to have the money for their own use. Finally, one of the grumblers made such a con-

OPPOSITE Two scenes from *The Triumphs of Caesar* by Andrea Mantegna (1431–1506).

163

The Roman Forum, seen
from the site of Caesar's
Basilica Julia.

spicuous scene that Caesar himself seized the man by the scruff of the neck and hauled him off for execution. In addition, he behaved with extraordinary savagery by arresting two other disaffected veterans – and offering them as human sacrifices to the war-god Mars. When his patience became exhausted, it was alarming how completely clemency was forgotten.

Even if the money would have been better spent on other things, Caesar could easily afford the vast expenditure involved in all these celebrations. The times when he had been hard put to it to find money were gone for ever; the victorious wars had made him enormously rich. In the traditional manner of great potentates, he spent a great deal of this wealth not only on celebrating Triumphs, but on erecting spectacular buildings. A great new hall for public business, the Basilica Julia, was going up in the Roman Forum; and next to that ancient meeting place a whole new Forum, the Forum Julium, had taken shape. As in other great Italian shrines, this complex of buildings was designed as a colonnaded precinct flanking and surrounding an imposing temple. It had originally been intended that this temple should be allocated to Venus the Victorious (Victrix), whose name had been Caesar's battle-cry at Pharsalus. But since Pompey, another great builder, had already completed another shrine dedicated to this aspect of Venus (beside his new theatre), Caesar now decided upon a revised dedication to Venus the Mother (Genetrix), since it was from this goddess, through the legendary Aeneas, that the Julian family claimed to be descended.

In the new temple there was a superb statue of Venus: and beside it Caesar placed a gilt-bronze statue of Cleopatra. She was able to see it with her own eyes: for shortly after the great Triumphs, the queen herself arrived in Rome. She came with her half-brother, the thirteen-year-old Ptolemy XIV, who was, in name, her fellow-monarch. And with her also was her recently born son Caesarion, whose presence enabled her to emphasise her claim that Caesar was the infant's father. The official purpose of this royal visit was to secure the confirmation of the treaty of alliance and friendship between Rome and Egypt, which her father had arranged with Caesar during his first consulship thirteen years earlier. Now he was consul once again, and dictator as well, and the treaty was duly reaffirmed. But the real reason why Cleopatra came to Rome was to resume her relationship with Julius Caesar, upon whose good will the whole future of Egypt and her regime depended.

Reconstruction of the interior of the Basilica Julia.

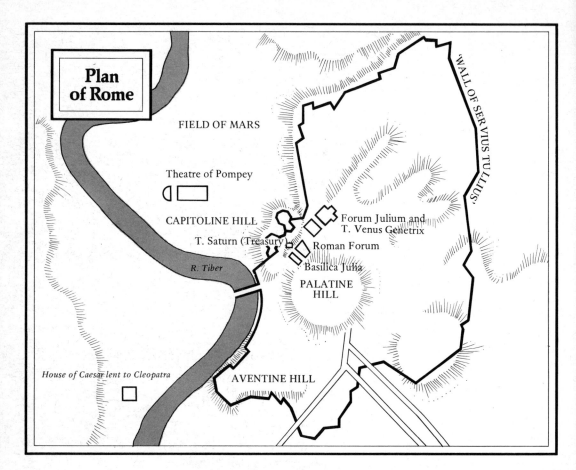

Plan of Rome

FIELD OF MARS

Theatre of Pompey

CAPITOLINE HILL

Forum Julium and
T. Venus Genetrix

T. Saturn (Treasury)

Roman Forum

R. Tiber

Basilica Julia

PALATINE
HILL

'WALL OF SERVIUS TULLIUS'

House of Caesar lent to Cleopatra

AVENTINE HILL

Moreover, his eye, according to some reports, may have been straying during the fifteen months since they had bidden farewell to one another at Alexandria. For he was reputed to have had an affair with a Mauretanian princess.

Nevertheless, he munificently lodged Cleopatra and her boy colleague, and her infant who may have been his own son, in a mansion that belonged to him on the right bank of the Tiber. There she no doubt maintained an impressive and spectacular court. The Romans who frequented it are mostly impossible to identify with any certainty, because, after her downfall and death sixteen years later, the leading Roman families were at great pains to deny that any such connexion had existed. Moreover, the only Roman whose first-hand record of her visit to Rome we possess (though even this only amounts to a few brief mentions) was Cicero; and Cicero hated her. He hated her because he disapproved of grandiose foreign queens. Besides, Cicero was a man who did not usually get on well

OPPOSITE Head of a woman perhaps identifiable with Cleopatra.

168

with women. And on this occasion he felt aggrieved because she had promised him a present and had failed to deliver it. Nevertheless, we can safely assume that many of the most eminent Romans, taking their cue from Caesar, flocked to attend upon her across the river.

When Caesar set up her statue in the temple of Venus Genetrix, this was wholly lacking in any Roman constitutional significance, since Cleopatra possessed no official standing in the city, except as a privileged ally. Nor did the gesture point to any present or future matrimonial relationship with Caesar, who was married already to Calpurnia, and belonged to a monogamous society, and in any case, according to Roman law, could not contract a marriage with a foreigner.

In the Greek east, it had long been habitual to set the effigies of kings and queens in temples, as honorary companions of the Olympian gods. Nevertheless, the conferment of this privilege upon Cleopatra in the Roman capital itself was a remarkable distinction, which surely indicated that she held a very special place in Caesar's esteem and affection. Whether Caesar, at the same time, placed it upon record that he was the father of her son Caesarion, we cannot be sure. But the complimentary treatment he accorded her must have ensured that her own assertions of his paternity received a great deal of respectful notice.

Reconstruction of the
Temple of the Divine
Julius Caesar in the Roman
Forum.

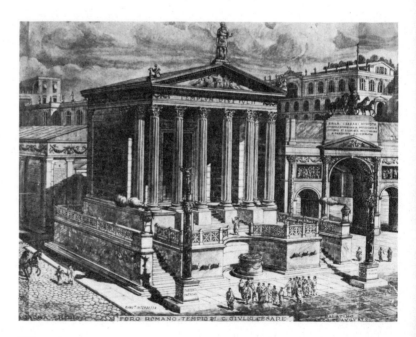

170

Cleopatra, while in Rome, seems to have exercised a certain influence upon the actions of Caesar. He may not have been as assiduously gallant to her as he had been in Alexandria, since he was exceedingly busy, and in addition his health was becoming undermined by all his warlike and administrative exertions. But it appears likely enough that a growing trend towards autocratic behaviour, which people were now noticing in the dictator, owed something to Cleopatra, to whose own Ptolemaic ideas the freedom of speech and action cherished by Roman Republican noblemen seemed ludicrous and undesirable. Moreover, we can identify certain specific, practical fields in which Caesar was indebted to Cleopatra's Alexandria, and therefore to herself, no doubt, as the principal intermediary.

OPPOSITE The ruins of Carthage, which Caesar rebuilt as a Roman colony.

For one thing, Caesar's introduction of certain religious rituals, relating to the god Dionysus (Bacchus), may be attributed to an Alexandrian origin, since this cult was the basis of the ruler-worship directed by Egyptians to their Ptolemaic monarchs. Secondly, Caesar's plan to establish magnificent public libraries at Rome was manifestly Egyptian, going back to the world-famous library of the Ptolemies at Alexandria. When, therefore, he entrusted this project to the great Roman polymath Varro (a former opponent in the Civil War), it may reasonably be assumed that Varro was assisted by advisers supplied by Cleopatra.

Furthermore, Caesar's ambitious projects for the construction of canals must surely have owed a good deal to Egypt, which was the very home and outstanding centre of this kind of irrigation. Helped once again, it may be assumed, by Cleopatra's experts, Caesar planned to dig a canal from the river Tiber, at a point near Rome, to Tarracina (formerly Anxur, the modern Terracina), in order to drain the malaria-stricken Pontine Marshes and form a new waterway; while the Fucine lake in the mountains east of Rome was also drained. In Greece, too, Caesar intended, no doubt with the same Egyptian inspiration behind him, to build a canal through the isthmus of Corinth, so that the Corinthian gulf, an extension of the Ionian Sea, would be directly joined to the Aegean on the other side of Greece. However, he did not live long enough for either scheme to come into effect. The completion of the Corinth canal had to wait until 1893. And as for the Pontine Marshes, in spite of numerous subsequent attempts to drain them, it was not until the years 1928–39 that the area was reclaimed in earnest.

But the most noteworthy of Caesar's Egyptian schemes, and the most durable of all his innovations in any and every sphere,

OVERLEAF Arcade a substructure of the late Republican Temple of Jupiter at Terracina (Anxur).

was his reform of the Roman calendar. The reason why Roman dates had so inconveniently advanced as much as two months ahead of the solar seasons was because Rome's calendar year (which was lunar, not solar) comprised only 355 days, instead of the requisite $365\frac{1}{4}$. To make up the balance, it had been customary to add a supplementary month in alternate years. However, in the course of the general breakdown of government during the later Republic, the insertion of these additional months had frequently been neglected; and that was how this discrepancy between the dates and the seasons had become so apparent.

Caesar decided to rectify the anomaly. To perform this delicate job he called in a certain Sosigenes, an eminent astronomer of Alexandria, who was surely recommended for the purpose by Cleopatra. The Hellenistic Greeks had undertaken a good deal of research into the various possibilities of establishing an effective, uniform calendar (hitherto unknown), and much of this work had been performed at the Alexandrian Museum, which was the leading intellectual centre of the Ptolemies. Indeed, one of their number, Ptolemy III, had tried nearly two centuries earlier to introduce a solar year, but this institution, although in theory it became more widely accepted, had never been put into practice on a large scale, until Caesar decided that it was time this should be done: and he, of course, was in a position to secure its implementation throughout all the vast territories of the Roman empire.

What he now did, with Sosigenes the Alexandrian as his guide, was to introduce a year of 365 days. Since however this fell a quarter of a day short of the actual solar year, he brought it up to the required average of $365\frac{1}{4}$ by the introduction in every fourth year (leap year) of an additional day. The new system was brought into operation by inserting two months of 29 and 28 days respectively between November and December 46 BC, so that this year – which had already received a supplementary month – attained the unique length of 445 days. Caesar's Julian calendar, as adjusted by Augustus and Pope Gregory XIII (1582), obtained widespread acceptance in the western world, and became statutory in England in 1752.

Somewhat inconsistently, in view of his own sexual reputation, Caesar allowed himself to be appointed Director of Public Morals (*praefectus moribus*), for a duration of three years. The title, with its vague and archaic ring, evidently seemed to him more suitable than the tougher-sounding dictatorship for certain social legisla-

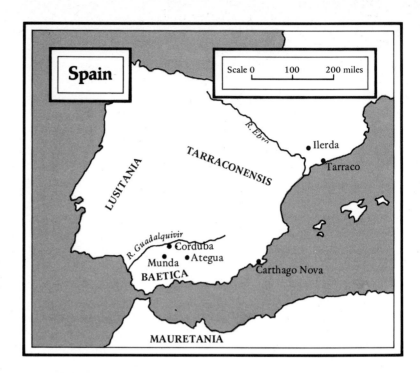

tion which he had in mind. He did not live long enough to reveal all his intentions in this field, but they seem to have included a further attempt, his third, to deal with the problem of debt. He also brought forward a series of measures intended to curb another abuse of the day, the ostentatious extravagence of the rich. Roman legislators had often suffered from the misapprehension that luxury could be curbed by legal enactments; and Caesar evidently felt the same, since he now attempted to frame laws to reduce this conspicuous outlay. These measures caused widespread alarm. It was one thing when inspectors were seen at the markets, controlling the prices of luxury goods. But it was also rumoured that they charged straight into the dining rooms of private houses, sometimes accompanied by soldiers, and if they saw too expensive foods being served, whisked them off the tables as the guests were actually eating them. Such gossip may not have been strictly accurate, but it shows the hostility with which these endeavours were regarded.

However, a halt had to be called to every project for Italy and the capital, because the civil war was still by no means over. For in

176

spite of the disaster sustained by the Pompeian cause at Thapsus in north Africa, it had now been vigorously revived in Spain. Four years earlier, Caesar thought he had stamped it out there. But since then he had made a bad choice of governors for the province, and when, after Thapsus, the surviving Pompeian commanders, under Pompey's elder son Cnaeus, managed to join up with one another in Spain, almost the whole of Baetica, the southern part of the country, came over to their side. Before long, they were able to raise yet another very substantial army, comprising thirteen legions and six thousand horse

Accordingly, early in November 46 BC, Caesar set out for Spain – for the fourth time in his life – and only twenty-seven days later he was already in Baetica, with a force comprising eight legions and eight thousand cavalry. For the campaign that followed we have to depend on a work known as the *Spanish War*. The unknown officer who wrote it was not as good as the chronicler of the Egyptian and African campaigns, but enables us to get some idea of the operations that now took place. Caesar was evidently eager to finish off the war as soon as possible. This was partly because his soldiers' patience was not inexhaustible; and he was experiencing great difficulty, during these winter months, in finding enough provisions and shelter for them. Besides, he himself was already looking ahead to another and far more glorious project, for he was eager to stop fighting his fellow Romans and to leave for the East, where he intended to conduct a major war against Parthia.

Nevertheless, as in north Africa, he did not find it at all easy to bring the Pompeians to battle. For two months they remained evasive. However, just as on that earlier occasion, he finally compelled them to abandon this successful policy. This he did by imperilling the city of Corduba (Cordova), a stronghold which played such an important part in his enemies' dispositions that they had felt obliged to garrison it with two legions under the command of Pompey's younger son Sextus. The threat to Corduba arose because, in mid-February of 45 BC, Caesar captured the well-stocked fortress of Ategua (Teba), which lay only twenty miles south east of the city. Cnaeus Pompeius tried to bring relief to his brother in beleaguered Corduba, but after the loss of Ategua he was obliged to recoil more than thirty miles towards the south-west, under hot pursuit from Caesar. Then, however, at an unidentifiable location named Munda, he was forced by the increasingly bad morale of his army to turn at bay.

OVERLEAF The ruins of Carthage.

The engagement that followed was a grim and horrifying one. Caesar's troops were eager to end the war once and for all, and when, at the outset, he called a halt in order to rectify the ragged dressing of the line, they felt great alarm; for they feared there was not going to be a battle after all. But there was, and for two hours it took the form of a series of charges and counter-charges, in which the superior training of Caesar's men was neutralised by an unfavourable slope. Florus, a minor historian of the second century AD, recounts a vivid incident.

When the two armies had long been cutting one another down, an unaccustomed disgrace presented itself to Caesar's eyes. His tired veterans gave ground, and though they had not gone so far as to flee, yet it was obvious that they were only resisting from shame and not from valour. Sending away his horse, Caesar himself rushed forward like a madman into the forefront of the battle, where he seized hold of those who were fleeing, heartened the standard-bearers, and dashed this way and that through the ranks, looking all round him, and gesturing, and shouting.

(Florus, *Epitome of Wars*, II, xiii, 80–5)

Yet finally, by a supreme effort, Caesar's tenth legion succeeded in driving in the enemy left, which then found itself subjected to a lethal rear attack from Caesar's Mauretanian cavalry. At this point, the entire Pompeian army, already disconcerted by a lateral troop movement by their own general Labienus – which they wrongly interpreted as a retreat – broke and fled.

While the result was still undecided, Caesar had become so depressed, according to rumour, that he even considered putting an end to himself. And later, when he had gained the victory, he turned to his staff and observed that this had been the toughest of all his battles: 'I have fought for victory often enough, but this is the very first time I have had to fight for my life.'

Thirty thousand Pompeian soldiers, it was said, met their deaths. Among them was Labienus. Cnaeus Pompeius, too, suffering from a wound and a sprained ankle, was caught and killed; and his severed head was taken to Hispalis (Seville) and displayed to its inhabitants – a gesture characteristic of a campaign accompanied by atrocities on both sides. But Sextus Pompeius got away once again, and lived on to become a thorn in the flesh of Caesar's successors.

After the battle, Caesar stayed on in Spain for a few months in order to reorganise its affairs, and by mid-September he was back in Italy once again.

OPPOSITE The colonnade of the Forum of Julius Caesar.

180

The Provinces of the
Roman Empire in 44 BC

He did not know it; but he had fought his last battle. And although he hoped to employ many of his soldiers again in his projected Parthian war, there were many more who had to be demobilised before the new operations began. Indeed, it was necessary to take this action very promptly, if a recurrence of the earlier mutinies, on a more serious scale than before, was to be avoided.

When legionaries had been discharged in the past, what they had wanted above all was land – and that was what they wanted again now, and what they had to be given. In consequence, Caesar proceeded to settle thousands of veterans, in allotments extended far and wide throughout Italy. Since, however, there was a limit to the amount of land that could be extracted from the inhabitants of the peninsula, he also founded a considerable number of citizen communities in the provinces. This had been done before, but only on a limited scale. Caesar, however, initiated at least forty such foundations, of which a number were actually brought to completion within his lifetime.

Many of these colonies were destined to have a glorious future – for example, those in the recently war-convulsed country of Spain: settlements which included Romula (the former Hispalis, now Seville), Tarraco (Tarragona) and Carthago Nova (Cartagena). And

182

in north Africa, too, the old Carthage, destroyed at the end of the Punic Wars a century earlier (146 BC), rose from its ashes as a Roman citizen community; and so did another great city which the Romans had destroyed in the same year, namely Corinth, which was to benefit from the projected new canal. There were other eastern colonies as well, though in these Greek-speaking countries the new foundations did little or nothing to Romanise the universal Hellenic culture of the local ruling classes. In the west, on the other hand, such colonies, in addition to half-way towns of 'Latin' status (in which not the whole community but the town councillors became citizens) were potent instruments of Romanisation.

The veteran legionaries who thus became colonists might be called upon, in times of crisis, to play their part in local defence; and meanwhile they served a useful purpose as active propagandists for Caesar. But the settlements were not intended for veterans alone. For a further remarkable feature of his colonising policy was the inclusion among the settlers of civilians too – including eighty thousand of the capital's destitute unemployed. Not only did this far-sighted scheme help to break down old stultifying barriers between Italians and provincials, but the inclusion of all these needy city-dwellers in the colonisation programme meant that Caesar, like no one else before him, had seriously begun to tackle the obstinate problem of the workless, depressed classes at Rome. During the years before his dictatorship, the recipients of grain in the capital, handed out by the government free of charge, had swollen to a total of 320,000. But now Caesar, owing to his policy of resettlement, was able to reduce this figure to less than half.

Moreover, the civilian settlers in the new foundations, however humble their origins and circumstances, were not intended to remain content with the role of proletarian passengers. On the contrary, in planning how these colonies should operate, Caesar broke through traditional prejudices altogether by allowing even ex-slaves to hold the annual elected offices, which had never been within their reach before.

Having tackled the problem of the urban unemployed, he also attempted to reduce worklessness throughout the Italian countryside. His method was to insist that, on the large ranches which in many parts of the peninsula had superseded the old small-holdings, at least a third of the labouring force should be free men and not slaves. This and certain similar measures, though praiseworthy as far as they went, did not lead to any permanent results, but only, perhaps, because Caesar did not live long enough to bring them

183

into effect. For he was only in power at Rome for an extremely short time. Yet this brief period was crammed with legislation, and improvement, and reform. No part of the programme was very revolutionary, and it did not look much beyond immediate necessities. But the measures were numerous and wide-ranging, and the speed at which they were rushed through roused constitutionalists such as Cicero to a variety of malicious comments and witticisms.

OPPOSITE Augustus in the robes of a priest.

But Caesar could not act all by himself: he needed the senate to help him. The senate he required, however, was not the old one, or its equally traditionalistic successor revived by Sulla, but a new body fitted to his own specification. Its numbers, therefore, were raised by one-third or more, from five or six hundred to nearly nine. Geographically, their distribution displayed a new breadth, for nearly half of the senators now came from outside Rome; only a very few of them, it is true, from the provinces – and those few from the most highly Romanised provinces such as southern Gaul – but an unprecedentedly large number from the municipalities of Italy. Bankers, industrialists and farmers, they represented Caesar's personal backing: and this broadening of the senate proved one of his most permanent achievements.

And if he arranged, as he did, that the senators should be the men he wanted, he also found ways to mould the leading offices of state to his own pattern. Under his direction as dictator, the annual elections to the consulships and other offices still continued. But he secured the passage of a law allowing him to 'recommend' quite openly to a large proportion of the more important posts – and indeed to fix who their holders should be, for a number of years ahead. In the old days the consuls had been rulers of the state. Now, they were convenient henchmen for Caesar: and their posts were appropriate ones to hand to loyal supporters as a recompense for their services. When, therefore, a consul died on the very last day of the year 45 BC, the dictator had a suitable man, Gaius Caninius Rebilus, whose turn it was to receive a reward of this kind, appointed to the vacant consulship for the remaining few hours of the year. Such actions not only involved telescoping the recognised procedure, but made the revered consular office into a bad joke – as Cicero complained to one of his correspondents.

At one o'clock Caesar announced the election of a consul to serve until 1 January – which was the next morning. So I can inform you that in Caninius' consulship no one had lunch. Still, nothing untoward occurred

185

while he was consul: such was his vigilance that throughout his consul-ship he did not sleep a wink.

Yes, you may laugh, but you aren't here. If you were, you could not help weeping. What if I told you everything? There are countless similar instances.

(Cicero, Letters to Friends, VII, 30)

Some junior officials, tribunes of the people, tried to oppose Caesar's torrent of measures, but all they succeeded in achieving was to exasperate him. And he had been infuriated too when Cicero wrote a panegyric on the arch-Republican, Cato, who had killed himself at the end of the north African campaign: for Caesar, though he carefully did not show his annoyance at the time, composed a venomous refutation. Yet he himself celebrated 'Liberty' on one of his coins; and he felt entitled to do so, because the programme he had in mind was peace and security for the empire, in which men could go about their business in prosperous calm. But what liberty meant to the traditional governing class was something entirely different from his version, namely their own right to uninhibited freedom of speech. And of that he was depriving them.

In the early months of 45 BC Cicero had planned to send him a memorandum showing how the restoration of the Republic should and could be planned. But by now he had given up the attempt, since obviously nothing would come of it. As he wrote to his friends, all the things worth having, things as dear as one's own children, had all totally disappeared: country, honour, respect, position, none of these possessed the smallest meaning any more.

For Caesar was as powerful as any king. The Roman kingship, abolished many centuries ago, had traditionally been treated by staunch Republicans as a thing of horror, the very negation of freedom. Yet now there were countless rumours that Caesar, who as a young man had boasted of his regal ancestry, was proposing to revive the institution in his own favour. In order to put an end to this gossip, he arranged for Antony, now restored to favour as his fellow-consul for 44 BC, to offer him a diadem publicly at a February festival, the Lupercalia, so that he himself could equally publicly reject it, thus denying that he had any ambition to become king.

But the word 'god', also, was being bandied round – once again in application to himself. Greek and other eastern monarchs had for centuries past been granted divine status by their own subjects, in recognition of their power, which, after all, was visibly greater

186

than that of any god. This seemed proper gratitude for services rendered, and conveyed the hope of even more lucrative benefits to come. Roman commanders, too, had been hailed as gods in the east, and so had Caesar: and now, after his sensational victories, the same term, in informal speech and unofficial cult, was being applied to him in the capital itself. But only the Roman state could pronounce deification, and Caesar was never officially declared a god – any more than he was declared to be king.

Had he lived on, it is possible that he might have introduced certain innovations regarding his own position in the state, to underline its uniqueness without having recourse to unpopular royal or divine appellations. Yet one may doubt whether he would have troubled to do any such thing. For the constitution did not interest Caesar very much. In him, the awed respect for constitutional niceties with which so many of his fellow Romans were imbued seems to have been almost totally lacking. It was enough for him that he was the absolute ruler. He stressed the point by placing his head on the metropolitan coinage, the first Roman ever to be thus portrayed in his lifetime. This innovation was somewhat ominous, because it reflected the longstanding practice of autocratic Greek monarchs; but it did not indicate any special constitutional powers. The only novelty he introduced into his official nomenclature, other than the label of Director of Public Morals, was the use of the title *Imperator* as a special, personal, permanent appellation, in order to show that he was the military commander who surpassed all other commanders.

But the constitutional basis of his rule remained the dictatorship, until the day of his death. It was a traditional office, but Caesar had already departed from all tradition when he accepted it for a duration of ten years. Then, in February 44 BC, he was appointed dictator for evermore – PERPETVO, as it is expressed on his coins. This was a really grave step to take, from the point of view of the Roman nobles, because the conversion of this essentially emergency post into a permanent autocracy meant that they themselves, however many consulships and other posts they might be permitted to hold, would never again be allowed to compete with him, or with one another, for the real control of the state, and all the pickings that went with it. It was at the time of this conferment, on 15 February 44 BC, that he so conspicuously rejected the diadem of kingship offered him by Antony. But the act of rejection was a publicity gesture without substance, since a diadem would not have made him any more powerful than he already was.

Then he brushed the question of his own position in the state aside – since his mind was occupied by entirely different matters. He had long been intending to carry out vast military operations in the east; and now he did not propose to wait any longer. For one thing, he was nearly fifty-six years of age, and not a very well preserved fifty-six at that. Twice during his latest campaigns, first at Thapsus and then again at Corduba, he had suffered from fainting fits, which may have been epileptic in origin. If he waited much longer, his power to command in the field might be seriously affected. Furthermore, he was utterly out of patience with the grudging, nagging attitude of the frustrated noblemen in the capital.

So all his plans were drawn up to leave Rome and go and fight against the Parthians. It was a pious duty, because they had defeated a Roman army, and killed Crassus, in 53 BC. But the enterprise was also prompted by the Roman aristocratic tradition of aggressive war and conquest as the highest human ambition, and in the case of Caesar himself, who was fully conscious of his own supreme military talents, these traditional aims were sharpened by a desire to rival and eclipse the conquests of Alexander the Great. He had forged his army into a more powerful, efficient and responsive martial instrument than the ancient world had ever seen before. And now this army must be used once again, not this time against fellow-Romans, nor against comparatively disorganised tribesmen such as the Gauls, but against the greatest foreign power that confronted the empire anywhere in the world, a power, moreover, which had inflicted a grave and humiliating defeat upon Rome. Once the Parthians were conquered, who knew whether Roman rule might not be extended to the Persian Gulf, or even, like the empire of Alexander, to the very borders of India itself?

So orders had now been given that sixteen legions, and ten thousand cavalry and archers, should be marshalled in the eastern provinces to await Caesar's arrival, when he would assume their supreme command. It was his intention to strike at the enemy from the north, across the upper Euphrates. However, a considerable force was first detached to deal with a potential European foe, the troublesome kingdom of Dacia, which had extended its power from Transylvania to the Black Sea. For once Caesar had suppressed the Parthians and expanded the Roman frontiers to the farthest east, it was believed that he intended to return through the Caucasus, and then wheel back across south Russia into Dacia, following the Danube as far as its junction with the Rhine and annexing further huge territories on the way.

The date for Caesar's departure was fixed: he was to leave Rome on 18 March 44 BC. When this deadline became known, its imminence brought to a climax the acute discontent which had been growing among the ranks of the Roman nobility. For whereas it was bad enough to be subjected to a perpetual dictator on the spot, it was a good deal worse to be governed by him while he was thousands of miles away. Indeed, as if to underline the point, he personally fixed all the major appointments to consulships and other offices, including the governorships of the provinces, for as long as two years ahead. But what angered them worst was the prospect of being governed by his henchmen when he was away. They might perhaps just tolerate the prospect of having to obey the official deputy (Master of Horse) he had appointed to succeed him in the city, a former consul named Marcus Lepidus – who in any case was due to leave for the western provinces before long. But what seemed peculiarly humiliating was the prospect of being

Caesar as Perpetual Dictator (DICT[ator] PERPETUO).

ordered about by Caesar's personal representatives in Rome, Oppius and Balbus. For they were not senators at all, but only knights; and yet they would be fully in a position to overrule, in their master's name, all the senators, and all the traditional officers of the state, including the consuls themselves.

OPPOSITE Marcus Brutus, the murderer of Caesar.

For the noblemen, this form of abject subordination, by remote control, seemed a dreadful prospect. Indeed, it was intolerable. In other words, Caesar had to be forcibly removed. There had been conspiracies or suggestions of conspiracies against his life before; but now plotting began in earnest. Its chief instigator was Gaius Cassius Longinus, who had come over to Caesar after Pharsalus, but had not, in his own view, been sufficiently rewarded. He was a proud and strong-tempered man, to whom subordination did not come easily:

> Age, thou art shamed!
> Rome, thou hast lost the breed of noble bloods!
> When went there by an age, since the great flood,
> But it was famed with more than with one man?
>
> (Shakespeare, *Julius Caesar*, I, 2)

Cassius won over his brother-in-law Marcus Brutus, who, like himself, had changed sides after Pharsalus. Although a very special protégé of Caesar who had long maintained affectionate relations with his mother, Marcus Brutus was an emotional, doctrinaire Republican, as befitted the supposed descendant of the Brutus famed for his liberation of Rome from the kings in the remote past. Another leading conspirator was Marcus Brutus' distant relation, Decimus Junius Brutus Albinus, who had served as one of Caesar's most important military subordinates, and was the recipient of his highest favours. With such men as these to act as their leaders, the various small separate groups of malcontents rapidly coalesced into a single body of sixty determined plotters.

Caesar was perfectly aware, of course, that many noblemen disliked him. It did not matter so much about young intellectuals and social figures like Catullus, although what he wrote was pretty offensive:

> Caesar, I have no great desire
> To stand in your good graces.
> Nor can I bother to enquire
> How fair or dark your face is.
>
> (Catullus, 93)

But Caesar knew perfectly well that the opposition was much more serious than that. When Cicero, for example, had been to call

191

After the murder of Caesar.
By J.D.Court (1797–1865).

on him one day, and was kept waiting in the anteroom, the dictator remarked: 'How can I doubt that I am heartedly disliked, when Cicero sits waiting and cannot visit me at his convenience? Yet if ever there was a good-natured man it is he. However, I am perfectly sure that he detests me.' And if he had no illusions about the feelings of Cicero, then surely he must have realised that other more violent members of the ruling class hated him too, and that their hatred presented the gravest of perils. Yet with a mixture of pride, contempt and fatalism he brushed the threat aside. Every senator, it is true, had sworn him an oath of personal allegiance. But that meant little – and after a senatorial delegation had visited him, one day, to recite a list of adulatory decrees, and he had provocatively failed to rise to his feet, the loyalty of the senate could be counted on even less. Meanwhile, however, Caesar took so little account of any personal danger that he even disbanded his personal guard of Spaniards; and when his friends urged him to bring them back into service, he would not take their advice.

On 15 March, only three days before he was due to depart from Rome and take command of his eastern armies, the senate held a meeting in a hall attached to Pompey's Theatre. The plot had not remained a complete secret, and as Caesar made his way to the meeting place someone thrust a warning note into his hand. But he still had not read it when he entered the hall. As he went in, there were gladiators outside, hidden from his view, but close at hand. Decimus Brutus had stationed them there, in case the conspirators needed them. Antony, a man of dangerously powerful physique, accompanied Caesar to the door, but was deliberately detained there in conversation by one of the plotters. Another of them, Tillius Cimber, came up close to him, ostensibly pleading for his brother's recall from exile, and took hold of his toga with both hands, pulling it away to throw him off balance. Then Casca struck the first blow with a dagger or metal pen, causing a slight wound in the neck, whereupon Caesar, turning sharply round, seized his weapon and held on to it. But in vain: as Plutarch tells us.

So it began, and those who were not in the conspiracy were so horror-struck and amazed at what was being done that they were afraid to run away and afraid to come to Caesar's help; they were too afraid even to utter a word. But those who had come prepared for the murder all bared their daggers and hemmed Caesar in on every side. Whichever way he turned, he met the blows of daggers and saw the cold steel aimed at his face and at his eyes ... for it had been agreed that they must all take part in this sacrifice, and all flesh themselves with his blood.

194

Because of this compact, Marcus Brutus also gave him one wound in the groin. Some say that Caesar fought back against all the rest, darting this way and that to avoid the blows and crying out for help, but when he saw that Brutus had drawn his dagger, he covered his head with his toga and sank down to the ground. Either by chance or because he was pushed there by his murderers, he fell down against the pedestal on which the statue of Pompey stood, and the pedestal was drenched with his blood: so that it seemed that Pompey himself was presiding over this act of vengeance against his enemy, who lay there at his feet, struggling convulsively under so many wounds.

(Plutarch, *Caesar*, 66)

Suetonius added a report that when Caesar saw the onslaught of Marcus Brutus, for whom he felt such an affection, he cried out in Greek: 'You, too, my child?' – and the alleged saying was linked with a rumour that Brutus, whose mother was so close to Caesar, was his illegitimate son.

Marcus Brutus commemorated his murder of Caesar by issuing a coin with daggers and the cap of Liberty – a specific reference to the Ides of March (EID. MAR.).

8
Caesar's Memory Lives On

THE CONSPIRATORS HAD ACHIEVED THEIR PURPOSE: but about what was to happen next they had made the gravest possible miscalculation. For once the tyrant was slain, they believed, the old Republic would automatically be restored. Not only, however, did this restoration not take place, but there was never any question that it should or would. Curiously blinkered by their own traditions, the Roman nobility just did not realise that they could not simply pick up the threads where it had dropped them at the beginning of the Civil War. For the power was no longer theirs to recapture: it had passed for ever into the hands of the general who could marshal the most formidable armed forces. These, clearly, were the legionaries who had served in Caesar's armies. And the men who could now command their loyalty were not Brutus and Cassius, but the supporters and successors of Caesar.

The first of these leaders to take charge was Antony, who had the advantage of occupying the consulship. Whether his funeral speech for Caesar was as emotional and inflammatory as Shakespeare's incomparable version is uncertain, and was already disputed in ancient times. What is sure, however, is that the funeral stimulated wild popular demonstrations: and for a brief period Antony reigned supreme. Taking forcible possession of Caesar's papers, he issued a stream of orders and regulations, for which he claimed the dead man's authority. He also went to Campania to superintend the settlement of colonies for Caesar's veterans – and collect six thousand of these men to serve as a personal bodyguard for himself. Meanwhile, coins were issued saluting the murdered dictator as Parent of his Country, and recalling the Clemency to other Romans for which he had made himself famous.

Lepidus, who had been designated Caesar's deputy during the first period of his forthcoming absence in the east, was in favour of taking immediate vengeance on the assassins. But Antony deflected this pressure by persuading him to leave immediately for the provinces which Caesar had assigned to him on the conclusion of his deputyship, namely Narbonese Gaul and Nearer Spain. For Antony had decided that disastrous conflict could only be avoided by a policy of moderation and compromise. In pursuit of this policy, he forcibly suppressed an excitable cult of Caesar's divinity that had sprung up in the Forum; and he passed a highly popular measure abolishing the title of dictator for all time to come. Moreover, he even allowed Marcus Brutus and Cassius to take up commands in the east – where Brutus issued an open challenge by striking coins which proudly commemorated the Ides of March.

PREVIOUS PAGE Statue of Julius Caesar.

198

Antony was as determined as Caesar had ever been to emerge ultimately as the universal autocrat. But for all his bluff manners he was an astute man, and at this stage he felt it was necessary to act with circumspection, since his own position was not yet fully assured. Its precariousness was at once demonstrated by the will Caesar had left behind him – in which Antony by no means occupied the central role. The provisions of the document, it is true, were, legally speaking, purely personal and not political at all, since the will of a Roman was only able to dispose of his own property, and could not aspire to assigning the headship of the Roman empire, a post which did not exist; and even existing offices of state were neither hereditary nor inheritable. Nevertheless, Caesar's will was of great importance, partly because his private estate was exceedingly large, and more particularly because the soldiers who had fought under Caesar would be very likely to transfer their allegiance to the man he designated as his personal heir.

The will turned out to provide something of a sensation. True, there was nothing surprising about the omission of Cleopatra's child, Caesarion (whether he was Caesar's son or not), because Roman law made it impossible for foreigners to receive testamentary bequests from Romans. But what attracted enormous,

199

Caesar, veiled as chief priest and described as Parent of his Country (PARENS PATRIAE).

astonished attention was Caesar's nomination, as his personal heir and the heir to three quarters of his possessions, of a young Roman who was still in his nineteenth year. This was Gaius Octavius, an outstandingly able, somewhat cold, young man, who was a great-nephew of Caesar, and had served with him in Spain. The will stipulated that, failing the birth of a male heir to Caesar's wife Calpurnia, Octavius should be adopted as his son. The remaining quarter of the dictator's estate was divided between two other relations, of relative obscurity. Various men were named in default of these three principal heirs, and among them were Decimus Brutus Albinus and Antony. The inclusion of Decimus, who had been one of the testator's assassins, created intense hostility against him, and he was glad to retire to the province Caesar himself had allotted to him, Cisalpine Gaul. As for Antony, he was deeply distressed that his own claims to be the main heir had been passed over; and but all he could do was to erect in the Forum a statue dedicated to Caesar as *The Glorious Parent*.

Meanwhile Octavius, ignoring all advice to the contrary, accepted his inheritance, and, as was correct for adopted sons, adopted the new designation of Gaius Julius Caesar Octavianus (rapidly dropping the last of these names altogether, though it is as Octavian that we speak of him today, before the later time when he came to be called Augustus). The rift between him and Antony rapidly widened, and before long, in 43 BC, the senate, eloquently egged on by Cicero, made Octavian, in spite of his extreme youth, one of the commanders of an army which was sent to fight Antony, and defeated him at Mutina (Modena). But then Octavian, slighted by the senate when it had second thoughts, made common cause with Antony and Lepidus, and the three men established the Second Triumvirate. This was not just an informal compact like the first, but officially perpetuated Caesar's autocracy, not, it is true, under one man any longer, but under this equally tyrannical committee of three. Cicero and many others were hunted to their deaths. Caesar on the other hand, like the mythical Romulus before him, was declared, in gratitude for his services, a God of the Roman state: so that Octavian was now a God's son. Then, at Philippi in Macedonia, the triumvirs overwhelmed the Republican army, and Brutus and Cassius met their deaths (42 BC). Octavian had sworn to avenge himself upon his adoptive father's assassins: and this was the first stage in the fulfilment of his oath.

OPPOSITE Augustus as a young man.

Many comments upon Caesar, recorded during these troubled first

two years after his death, have come down to us. The conspirators had not brought Cicero into their plot, since they were afraid he might talk. Nevertheless, he exultantly applauded the Ides of March – though he wished they had killed Antony as well. In his work *On Duties*, written at this time, he explained why the dictatorship had been altogether intolerable – because absolute rule was the most hideous imaginable crime.

Cicero's condemnation of the tyrant, echoing ancient Greek eulogies of tyrannicide, had abundant after-effects, reverberating down the ages. But in the years just after Caesar's death there were those who still took a very different view of him. For example, when one of the dictator's close associates, Gaius Matius, was approached by Cicero for support, his dignified reply refused to discredit the memory of his old friend.

I am well aware of what people have said against me since Caesar's death. They reproach me with my sorrow at the passing of an old friend, and indignation at the death of one I loved. They assert that patriotism should be put above friendship, as though they had already proved that Caesar's removal had benefited the State. But I will not try to be clever: I confess that I have not attained to their heights in philosophy. ...

I will not go out of my way to give offence – apart from deploring the sad end of a dear friend of mine and a most distinguished man.

([Cicero], *Letters to Friends*, XI, 28)

'If Caesar,' Matius had been heard saying, 'with all his genius, could not find a way out, who will now?' There were others who did not so openly defend Caesar, but who likewise did not feel able to revile his memory like Cicero: men who wanted desperately to remain neutral or independent. One of them was the distinguished historian and literary patron Pollio, who wrote to Cicero that, although when he obeyed Caesar he was only acting under orders, he nevertheless obeyed them with a sense of deep devotion and loyalty.

After the deaths of Brutus and Cassius, the Roman empire was divided between Antony, who had distinguished himself at Philippi, and Octavian, who had not. Antony, as senior partner, was able to choose which regions he should rule, and selected the east. There he took over Caesar's role as Cleopatra's lover, and felt obliged to support her claim that Caesarion was Caesar's son. Octavian, who, eliminating Sextus Pompeius and Lepidus, controlled the western empire and resided at Rome, naturally did not welcome the implications of this claim upon his own position, and laid great emphasis upon his personal adoption in the dictator's will, describing himself on his coins as 'Son of the Divine Julius'. Finally, after prolonged political, naval and military manoeuvrings, Antony was decisively defeated by Octavian in the sea-battle of Actium in 31 BC. In the next year, Antony and Cleopatra committed suicide, and Octavian, on being advised that 'a multiplicity of Caesars is not a good thing', had Caesarion killed. During the intervening years, a number of the surviving assassins of Caesar had joined Antony's cause, and now Octavian put them to death too. And this completion of his vengeance upon the killers of his adoptive father was duly celebrated by the dedication of a Roman temple to Mars the Avenger.

Yet Octavian, who now took the solemn name of Augustus, was faced with a grave dilemma. On the one hand, he rightly regarded it as impossible to restore a freely working Republic. In effect, therefore, an autocracy as wholehearted as Caesar's had to be maintained. And yet the murder of Caesar warned the new ruler in unmistakable terms what would happen to himself if he perpetuated Caesar's autocracy in equally naked and unconcealed form. What he did, therefore, in order to have the best of both these worlds, was to create an elaborate and highly subtle system according to which the power, and the troops who provided it, remained in his own hands, while at the same time traditional institutions were meticulously revived so that it was even possible to assert that the Republic had been restored. To us, the fiction sometimes seems threadbare. But to most Romans, who, for all their Republicanism, had been converted by decades of anarchy to a pressing awareness of the need for order, it seemed satisfactory enough. Behind this careful façade Augustus conducted that far-reaching overhaul of the entire governmental system which Caesar had not had the time to make – and perhaps not the inclination either.

In such an ostensibly restored Republic, the memory of Caesar took on a somewhat equivocal appearance. The actual events of his career, which had included so much violence and illegality, were glossed over or left veiled in silence, while Augustus' official propaganda, which was a markedly successful feature of his regime, stressed the divinity posthumously conferred on the dictator by the Roman state, and his adoptive fatherhood – described as plain fatherhood – of Augustus who had so triumphantly avenged him. The great Augustan writers interpreted this

ABOVE AND FAR RIGHT
Bronze coin of Octavian
(CAESAR DIVI F[ilius] – son
of a god) in honour of the
deified Caesar (DIVOS
IULIUS).

LEFT A Roman warship. The crocodile, emblem of Egypt, suggests that the ship took part in the battle of Actium.

situation in various acceptable ways of their own choice. Virgil's earlier poem, the *Georgics*, had interpreted the murder of Caesar as a cosmic disaster. But now, in his last work the *Aeneid*, the only mention the dead man receives already implies a certain diminution or disparagement of the actual facts of his career. For it was up to Caesar, the poet makes Aeneas' father Anchises suggest, to take the initiative, owing to his famous clemency, in bringing the civil war with Pompey to an end: in other words, it had been his fault that the war had ever begun.

> You be the first
> In mercy, you who trace your line from Olympus
> And have my blood in your veins – cast
> down your weapons!
>
> (Virgil, *Aeneid*, VI, 834f)

In the poems of Horace, Virgil's younger contemporary, the only reference to Caesar – apart from eulogies of Augustus' role as avenger – is an allusion to the Star of Julius, that comet which had been seen taking the deified ruler's soul up to the heavens, purged of all earthly stain so that the irregularities of his lifetime were no longer of any relevance. Another poet, Ovid, roundly declared that the greatest of all Caesar's deeds had been his fathering of Augustus. The historian Livy went further still along the path of depreciation, for he put the question whether the birth of Caesar had been more of a curse or a blessing to the world. Indeed, although his description of the Civil War has not survived, his attitude to Caesar was evidently so lukewarm that Augustus described him as a 'Pompeian' – though without, it is significant to note, withdrawing his patronage from Livy's History.

Nevertheless, the same ruler, while describing himself not of course by the hated, abolished title of dictator, but by the vague and tactful designation of *princeps* (leading citizen), retained the name of 'Caesar' in his nomenclature. Its retention was indispensable because of the great popularity of his memory with the legions. Moreover, when Augustus adopted his younger relatives, they took on the same name, too, and it was as Tiberius Caesar that his stepson came to the throne in AD 14.

In his reign, the historian Cremutius Cordus was deemed (unlike him) to have gone over the invisible line of permissibility when he eulogised Brutus and hailed Cassius as the 'last of the Romans'; and these descriptions helped to bring about his enforced death. The next emperor but one, Claudius, of the same

Coin of Augustus, showing on one side the comet which declared the deification of Caesar (DIVUS IULIUS).

Claudian family as Tiberius, had never been adopted into Caesar's Julian house. Yet upon his accession, he too assumed the name of Caesar, which had thus completed the process of transformation into an imperial title. And then Nero, whom he adopted, became Caesar as well. When he ascended the throne, his chief minister Seneca expressed strong disapproval of Caesar's assassination – since his own master, too, often seemed all too likely to incur the same fate, and reprobation of the murder of autocrats had thus become essential.

Seneca's nephew was the poet Lucan, whose ten-book epic masterpiece the *Civil War*, generally known as the *Pharsalia*, described the struggle between Caesar and Pompey, culminating in the latter's defeat and death. One of the most remarkable features of Lucan's poem is his change of attitude towards Caesar as the work proceeds. At first the dictator is regarded with neutrality, tempered by an appreciation of his great gifts. But then, from the third book onwards, this cautious attitude is replaced by an intense hatred. On looking back at the Civil War, Lucan now

truly sees Pompeius Magnus as deserving of his title 'Great', and
Caesar on the other hand as the villain, whose 'swords reeked with
slaughter and with guilt', as he perpetrated every kind of cruelty
and depravity. This change of approach corresponded with
Lucan's growing disillusionment with the tyrant of his own day,
Nero: and Nero, in the end, retaliated by compelling him to commit
suicide, for alleged participation in a conspiracy. This was in
AD 65, and earlier in the same year a certain Gaius Cassius
Longinus had been charged with revering the statue of his ancestor
Cassius as 'Leader of the Cause'.

Not long afterwards the suicide of Nero brought the house of
Caesar and Augustus, the Julio-Claudian dynasty, to an end. Yet
his successor Galba (AD 68–9), though belonging to another noble
clan altogether, took the names of both of his great forerunners,
thus recognising that these were designations not merely of a
single dynasty but of any and every emperor. When he appointed
another aristocrat, Piso Licinianus, as his own son and heir, this
young man too was named Caesar. But Galba and Piso were killed,
and the nominee of the Roman army in Germany, Vitellius, when
in his turn he claimed the throne, innovated by refusing the name
or title Caesar, and instead calling himself Germanicus, after the

208

legions who had given him the throne. During the Civil Wars of this period, the coins issued by the contesting armies made great play with the name of the dictator. Some of these issues portrayed him with honour as 'the army's man', while others, on the contrary, revived Brutus' exultant type of the Ides of March, now that another tyrant, Nero, was likewise dead.

Under the 'Flavian' dynasty which was next founded by Vespasian, the imperial nomenclature adopted a standard double prefix *Imperator Caesar*, and princes destined for future occupancies of the throne were distinguished by the single name of 'Caesar'. Portrait-busts of the dictator continued to be made in considerable numbers. Yet when Vespasian's sons Titus and Domitian issued coinages reviving the designs of their great predecessors, Caesar was not among those who were honoured. This was remedied, however, by Trajan (AD 98–117), whose own similar 'restoration' issues paid more attention to Caesar than to any of the other great figures of the past. For Trajan himself was another aggressive, expansionist, military man, whose conquests invited analogies with the first of the Caesars. Such comparisons had become less invidious by his day, since the old Republicanism, which had hitherto survived in certain quarters, was at last defunct.

TOP Galba (AD 68–9), the first Emperor to have no connection with the Julian house, nevertheless used the title CAESAR.
ABOVE Julius Caesar honoured on a coin of another great conqueror, the Emperor Trajan (AD 98–117).

The writers of the period did not speak about Caesar with one voice. Tacitus mentioned him very often, and never with the dispraise reserved, for example, for Augustus, whose clever fictions he distrusted. Suetonius, on the other hand, who usually leaves his readers to make their own final judgments, concludes about Julius Caesar, that 'his other [bad] actions and words so turn the scale, that it is thought he abused his power and was justly slain'. Yet at the same time Suetonius implied a less negative judgment when he designed his collection of biographies as 'The Twelve Caesars' – starting with Julius. For this title and framework suggested that the dictator was no mere destroyer or transitional figure, but chief founder of the imperial system and line.

Suetonius' contemporary Plutarch, though he did not understand the dictator very well, felt the same. Nevertheless, Plutarch was also firmly convinced that Caesar's autocracy had been evil: 'what made him most openly and mortally hated was his passion to be king' – and the only fruits of all his endeavours were an empty name, and a glory that made him envied and hated. For although a loyal supporter of the Roman emperors of his own day, Plutarch remained a Greek, who looked back nostalgically at the past age of

209

small Greek city states and a relatively modest Roman Republic –
and he censured Caesar as the destroyer of these historic institutions. Both Suetonius and Plutarch, following the principles of
Greek tragic drama, noted carefully the signs of arrogance and
hybris that portended the dictator's downfall, especially in his
final years. And both reflected the widespread ancient view that
he had been, above all else, the man who gambled with fortune:
the man who was never afraid to throw down enormous stakes.

After Septimius Severus had conquered his rivals after bloodthirsty civil wars, he told an alarmed senate that Pompey and
Caesar had come to grief because their clemency, in the course of
similar disturbances, had been overdone (AD197). Severus' younger
contemporary, the Greek historian Dio Cassius, supported Caesar,
taking his side against Cicero, and refusing Brutus and Cassius
their title of 'Liberators' – because one man rule was a necessity.
Meanwhile, as a third-century papyrus from Dura-Europus on the
Euphrates reveals, the army still continued to honour each
recurrent anniversary of Caesar's deification.

But the emperor Julian the Apostate (AD 361–3), in his *Caesars*
which offers a humorous sketch of his forerunners, says of the
dictator that his one aim was to gain the supremacy for himself –
'such was his passion for glory that he seemed ready to contend
with Zeus himself for dominion'. Saint Augustine's pupil Orosius,
on the other hand, in spite of the anti-pagan intention of his history,
declared that Caesar 'was destroyed in the effort to build the
political world anew in the spirit of clemency, contrary to the
example of those who had gone before him'. And a fifth century
calendar known as the Fasti of Silvius still includes the dictator's
birthday among the very few ancient anniversaries of which it
takes note.

In the first centuries of the Byzantine empire, 'Caesar' continued
to be one of the emperor's titles, and it was retained thereafter to
designate the highest rank after the imperial dignity itself. Meanwhile, in the west, Charlemagne had seen himself as the new
Caesar, and the men who subsequently reigned over the Holy
Roman Empire employed the title, in the German form of Kaiser.
In Bulgaria, too King Simeon, in imitation of the Holy Roman
Empire, employed the same designation of Tsar. And so it was, in
the words of Edward Gibbon, that the title of Caesar, like the title
of Augustus, 'has been preserved from the fall of the Republic to
the present time.'

As the supposed founder of the Roman empire, and thus the

founder of the Holy Roman Empire which claimed to be its successor, Julius Caesar was now regarded as a semi-divine figure: if only he had been a Christian, he would almost have been the patron saint of Europe. Moreover, as the imperial founder, he came to symbolise the principle of legitimacy. Throughout the Middle Ages, he was not thought of as inventing a new form of government. Indeed, his supersession of the Republic scarcely interested this epoch, which, on the whole, envisaged ancient Rome not as a Republic but as an empire – so that many chronicles jump straight from the last antique monarch, Tarquin the Proud, to Julius Caesar, omitting Republican times altogether.

William of Poitiers, who had studied Suetonius, saw William the Conqueror of England as a second and greater Caesar. Then, in the twelfth century, the *Commentaries* began to appear in the great libraries, as their surviving catalogues reveal. At first, this influence of Caesar's writings remained only slight, but William of Malmesbury made use of them in his *History of the English Kings*, and the *Gesta* (Deeds) of the Archbishops of Trier employed them freely. John of Salisbury (d. 1180), with over-ambitious contemporaries in mind, condemned both Caesar and Alexander as tyrants who misused their natural talents through an excessive desire for glory. But the Emperor Frederick II (d. 1250) was proud to regard himself as Caesar's reincarnation. The Russians, on the other hand, had at first regarded the Byzantine emperor as the Caesar (Tsar) par excellence, since he was considered the head of the Orthodox Christian world. When, however, the Tartars conquered Russia and their Khan became its ruler, he was referred to as 'Tsar' in

Constantine the Great (AD 306–337) still stressed the titles CAESAR and AUGUSTUS.

211

Russian documents, and that was how the great series of Russian Caesars began. In 1346 Stephen Dushan of Serbia assumed the same style.

Meanwhile, in the west, there was a literary fashion for the Cult of the Nine Worthies, famous men of history and legend: and Julius Caesar was one of them. When Dante depicted Lucifer in the depths of the Inferno, the three mouths of the monster are seen crunching not only Judas Iscariot, but Brutus and Cassius too. For being a supporter of the Holy Roman Empire of his own day, which existed, he believed, by virtue of the will of God, Dante saw the ancient Roman empire as its direct forerunner, so that the murderers of Caesar were destroyers of a god-sent dispensation. Nevertheless, Dante did not forget the shadow of Caesar's arch-enemy Cato, whom he interpreted as the model of antique pagan virtue, placing the shore beneath the Mount of Purgatory under his guardian care.

Subsequently, Petrarch, devoted to the worship of fame, dwelt on Caesar in his Latin *Lives of Illustrious Romans,* and then devoted a fuller biography to him alone and to his deeds. For the humanists of the fourteenth and fifteenth centuries expended great time and energy upon reconstructing the figures of the Roman great. King René of Anjou included a blazon of Caesar in his heraldry, and attention to the dictator's memory became closer still after the *Commentaries* had been published in Rome in 1469, and after they had subsequently been translated into the principal western languages. Although it was recognised to be impossible, after reading Cicero, Sallust and Lucan, to carry the idealisation of Caesar beyond a certain limit, works of art displaying his deeds now abounded. They included a very popular contemporary medallion (still widely sold today as a genuine ancient coin) displaying the inscription 'I came, I saw, I conquered' in Latin within a wreath.

Since the early Renaissance, in its obsessively keen study of the ancients, was stirred by their military achievements more than anything else, there were many depictions of Caesar's battles, and his spectacular Triumphs, too, provided a particularly fertile theme. As Alfonso I of Aragon entered the conquered city of Naples in 1443, he refused a laurel crown because he did not venture to compare himself to Alexander or Caesar, but at his Triumph there appeared an actor with Caesar's crown and toga. When Borso d'Este, Duke of Modena and Reggio (Emilia), proceeded on a triumphal tour nine years later, a scene was enacted in which Caesar, attended by seven nymphs, offered his blessing to

212

the prince. Then, for Francesco Gonzaga the young marquis of Mantua, Andrea Mantegna painted the *Triumphs of Caesar* (1485–92) which are now to be seen at Hampton Court.

A triumphal arch erected in honour of the Borgia Pope Alexander VI (1492–1503) was inscribed with the words: 'Rome was great under Caesar, but now she is greater. Alexander VI reigns: Caesar was a man, but the Pope is God'. The dictator was also the idol and dream of Alexander's son Cesare Borgia, Duke of Valentinois, who in 1500, boldly inviting comparisons with his own exploits, presented a spectacular Triumph of Caesar with a procession of eleven magnificent chariots. Two years later, in honour of the marriage of his sister Lucrezia, the people of Rome arranged a procession of thirteen chariots illustrating the Triumphs of ancient heroes – with special reference to Hercules and Caesar. In 1513, Florence, too, organised a Triumph, to honour the elevation of its duke's brother to the papacy as Leo X: and on the fourth chariot, which represented Caesar's victory in the Alexandrian War, the nineteen-year-old painter Pontormo had depicted the dictator's most famous deeds.

Machiavelli, on the other hand, was very critical of Caesar, pronouncing him in the *Discourses on the First Decade of Livy* (1516–9) to be 'the first tyrant in Rome, so that the city was never free again'. He was more detestable than Catiline, declared Machiavelli, and had ruined Rome utterly, in sharp contrast to the legendary founder Romulus, who had done everything to improve it. Caesar, added Machiavelli, had initially founded his power on the favour of the people, whom he won over by extravagant liberality – but if he had lived on, he would have been obliged to moderate his expenditure, or he must inevitably have fallen. Renaissance scholars in general took the same sort of view, seeing the dictator as the archetype of reckless ambition who strode through battle and destruction to a bloody grave. Brutus, on the other hand, seemed 'the last of the Romans', and it was in this heroic spirit that Michelangelo devised his portrait bust (c. 1542). In France, Marc-Antoine Muret (1546) and Jacques Grévin belonged to a long series of French dramatists who wrote tragedies about Caesar. Meanwhile, Erasmus, although maintaining that the best of all constitutions is monarchy and the worst is its perversion into tyranny, had recommended carefully selected passages from the *Commentaries* for school reading; and subsequently Ascham recommended that English pupils should study these works for the sake of their language, 'without all exception to be made either

213

A scene from *The Triumphs of Caesar* by Mantegna (1431–1506).

by friend or foe'. It was tempting, however, to read them in English instead, for in 1565 one of our most attractive translators, Arthur Golding, had produced a complete version of the *Gallic War*, which superseded a partial rendering made thirty-five years earlier.

At least five late Elizabethan playrights offered portraits of Caesar. One of them was Thomas Kyd (1593): many countries, he declared, are full of dead men's bones by Caesar slain.

> Th'infectious plague, and Famine's bitterness,
> Or th' Ocean (whom no pity can assuage),
> Though they contain dead bodies numberless,
> Are yet inferior to Caesar's rage.
>
> > (Kyd, *Cornelia*, Act IV, Scene 1)

That is on the lines of the later books of Lucan, who had come to interpret Caesar as an evil destroyer. And other Elizabethans portrayed him as an inflated boaster and braggart, like the Hercules of Lucan's uncle Seneca.

Shakespeare, in his earlier plays, often referred to the dictator, mingling awed admiration of his gifts with mocking censure of his arrogance. *Julius Caesar* (1599) was the first of the plays that he based mainly upon Plutarch's *Lives*. He had read Plutarch in English translations by Thomas North, who in turn had based his renderings on French versions by Jacques Amyot. Shakespeare presents Caesar as he appears to the conspirators. Once more, we find the boaster of Senecan tradition, assimilated with a power-drunk stage conqueror like the Tamerlane of Marlowe – brought onto the stage merely in order to be killed, and to display the classic, Nemesis-inspired, fall of a great prince. Shakespeare's Caesar is arrogant, pompous and superstitious. Of his courtesy, breeding, charm, heroic large-mindedness, humour, little trace is to be seen. Was this, then, the man that did awe the world? And yet if this Caesar is only a shadow of the real or even the Plutarchian Caesar, Shakespeare's Brutus is a faithful portrayal of the Brutus of Plutarch, presented with a superbly expressed profundity of feeling that was far beyond Plutarch's capacity. Voltaire said the play ought to have been called, not *Julius Caesar*, but *The Tragedy of Marcus Brutus*. Yet for all Caesar's personal hollowness, his presence, and then his departed presence, continues to hang heavily over the whole play.

To Francis Bacon, Lord Verulam (d. 1626), Caesar was 'the most complete character of all antiquity'. Then, between 1651 and 1829,

216

he was made the hero of at least twenty operas, including four or five describing his death, and eight relating to his adventures in Egypt. The eighteenth century witnessed many lavishly illustrated editions of the *Commentaries*. 'Caesar possesseth this almost peculiar to himself,' remarked Henry Felton in 1715, 'that you see the Prince and the Gentleman as well as the Scholar and the Soldier in his memoirs.' Montesquieu, however, believed that 'Caesar's bloody robe plunged Rome into servitude': though he conceded that, even if Caesar and Pompey had never existed, the Roman state would still have fallen, for there would have been other ambitious men to destroy it.

To the American and French revolutionaries, too, it was natural that Brutus the tyrannicide should exercise a much greater appeal than Caesar the tyrant. As one of the Americans, Patrick Henry, was heard to cry with satisfaction, 'Caesar had his Brutus!' And William Blake, writing in 1789 full of high hopes of the French Revolution, declared:

> The strongest poison ever known
> Came from Caesar's laurel crown.

The followers of Napoleon, for all their revolutionary origins, were bound to develop quite a different view. In 1800, Lucien Bonaparte distributed a work which he himself may have written, entitled *A Parallel between Caesar, Cromwell, Monck and Bonaparte*. Napoleon, he declared, was Caesar's equal as a military commander, and his superior as a politician – because he favoured orderly society and the educated class, whereas Caesar had encouraged disorderliness and debtors. Napoleon himself, though the heavily Romanised portraits his artists made of him were reminiscent of Augustus rather than Caesar, believed that every general ought to read the *Commentaries* as part of his education. In exile at St Helena, he dictated to Count Marchand his *Summary of the Wars of Caesar*, containing the forthright judgments of one exceptional commander upon another.

Meanwhile, however, Benjamin Constant, fastening upon the now commonplace analogy between the emperor of the French and the dictator of Rome, had employed the comparison to the discredit of both, speaking ill of Napoleon, by whom he had been banished, and remarking that when Caesar's soldiers had marched at his orders, their action had disgraced and profaned his forebears' tombs. Another who compared the two leaders was Lord Byron. Although he felt Caesar's versatility to be so astonishing

Julius Caesar on horseback; tapestry.

that 'nature seems incapable of such extraordinary combinations', his conclusion in *The Island* (1823) remains adverse:

> Had Caesar known but Cleopatra's kiss,
> Rome had been free, the world had not been his.
> And what have Caesar's deeds and Caesar's fame
> Done for the earth? We feel them in our shame:
> The gory sanction of his glory stains
> The rust which tyrants cherish on our chains.

In general, however, the reputation of Caesar had been rising, among the friends and enemies of Napoleon alike. For the growing romanticism of the age could not fail to be fascinated by such men of destiny, and they were exalted once again by the quasi-theological analysis of Hegel, who, interpreting the Prussian monarchy as society's final expression of Rousseau's General Will, saw Caesar as the Hohenzollerns' mighty forerunner, 'the paragon of the Roman adaptation of means to ends' (1823–7). Michelet, on the other hand, exalted Caesar as 'the man of humanity', the reformer who helped the man in the street; while Macaulay believed that the words he wrote early in the Civil War, when he declared that there was nothing he wanted more than that his enemies should be like themselves and he like himself, were the finest ever written.

But meanwhile in France the ambitions of Louis Napoleon were emerging, and in 1841 the Count de Champagny, seeing the writing on the wall, praised Caesar for one thing only: for the warning his career supplied about the terrible dangers of autocratic government. In 1848 Louis Napoleon was elected president, and four years later he became the Emperor Napoleon III. In 1850 François Romieu put forward a theory and justification of what was now called, perhaps for the first time, Caesarism. This he defined as the régime of a prince brought to supremacy by the people and invested with absolute power – a phenomenon which he described as the inevitable result of culture, scepticism, and rationalistic thought. The term Caesarism was used constantly in order to compare the Napoleons with Caesar, to their credit and discredit alike. Yet the contrast it implied between legitimate monarchy and popular military autocracy was foreign to Greco-Roman thought and practice, and thus anachronistic in application to Caesar, who, in any case, was no social revolutionary. Napoleon I, no doubt, shared certain qualities of leadership and genius with the Roman. But, as Karl Marx observed, to bracket Caesar with Napoleon III is like comparing the High Priest Samuel with the Archbishop of Canterbury. Meanwhile Napoleon III himself, of whom Trollope said 'we cannot take the facts as the emperor of the French gives them to us', frankly admired Caesar's autocracy and aggression; although he erected a monument to Vercingetorix as well. He also sponsored surveys and excavations relating to the Gallic War, which contributed a good deal to archaeological knowledge of the principal campaigns.

However, the greatest of all Roman historians Theodor Mommsen, in the third volume of his *Roman History* (1856), did not compare even Napoleon I to Caesar, but contrasted them – in favour of the latter, who had never, he reminded his readers, needed Napoleon's brutal coup of 18 Brumaire to win his supremacy. In the following year Mommsen even more explicitly dissociated Caesar from the prevailing theory of Caesarism, implying that the great man's whole story completely transcended this concept as, in the light of recent French history, it was nowadays understood. Mommsen's unbounded admiration of the dictator owed much to the circumstances of contemporary Germany, in which, with the historian's strong approval, the aristocratic Junkers had been subordinated to the Prussian monarchy; and Mommsen believed that Caesar had been trying to do just the same. In contrast to Cicero whom he despised, he saw Caesar as a great innovator, a legislative genius determined to give the lower orders of the community social justice, a saviour of society who felt true kingly greatness within his breast, a new Alexander the Great who understood how to identify his personal interests and ambitions with the fulfilment of a universal purpose. Julius Caesar, he declared, was 'the sole creative genius produced by Rome, and the last produced by the ancient world'. Having asserted so much, he found he had to bring his Roman history to a stop, for there was nothing left to say about Augustus.

Mommsen exercised a powerful spell. Yet, in the long run, his version failed to command acceptance. He was right to detach Caesar from Caesarism, and his French nationalist critics, who opposed his view by declaring that the Gauls would have evolved just as successfully if they had never been conquered, were probably wrong. But his emphasis on the dictator as a superman of destiny, the resolver of political dilemmas by the creation of a novel constitutional form, was not wholly acceptable. Mazzini, in 1865, took the opposite view: that Caesar (like Napoleon I) did not begin a period of history but ended one. Eduard Meyer, on the other hand, in his *History of Antiquity* (1884–1902), agreed with Mommsen that he was a great originator, but believed that what he was aiming at was the creation of a new monarchical state on Hellenistic lines – a view which, in its turn, has incurred criticism, since in spite of Cleopatra he was by no means as Hellenised as all that.

The first decades of the twentieth century added some interesting though scarcely fundamental contributions. C.W.C.Oman, re-marking that Caesar the altruist is a nineteenth century fiction (of which Mommsen was not guiltless), already, well before the two world wars – he was writing in 1902 – saw how perilous it was to regard Caesar's forcible assumption of supreme power as a matter of congratulation. Four years later, on the other hand, Bernard Shaw's play *Caesar and Cleopatra* portrayed Caesar with a good deal of sympathy, as a figure of lofty magnanimity, austere and essentially alone, in sharp contrast to Cleopatra, who is quite misleadingly presented as a frivolous child. Then, in spite of the rise and fall of a would-be new Caesar in Wilhelm II, F. Gundolf wrote *Caesar: The History of his Fame* (1924), translated from the German under the title of *The Mantle of Caesar*, in which his hero was presented in extravagant terms as the supreme symbol and ideal of the eternal, absolute dominator, mystically present and operative throughout all the intervening ages. In the light of what has happened during the half-century since he wrote, his topical comments are worth recalling: 'Our era is shrieking for the man of might. We can witness Germany entrusting her destinies to any slightly visionary talent. . . .' – who will be markedly inferior to the magnificent Caesar.

Since then, studies of Caesar have continued to abound. F.E.Adcock's depiction of him in the *Cambridge Ancient History* (volume IX, 1932) is an implied criticism both of Gundolf and of Meyer, according to which Caesar is interpreted, perhaps too narrowly, as a Roman and a traditionalist. M. Rambaud has subjected the *Commentaries* to unprecedentedly sharp censure, seeing them not only as propaganda but as lies. Finally, Stefan Weinstock (1971) has presented Caesar as a bold religious reformer, who seized the chance of the honours lavished upon him by the senate to work out, as he went along, a new kind of autocratic theology, and who, at the moment of his death, was on the very point of establishing a Roman monarchy based on ruler-cult.

It is not altogether surprising that Caesar's life has been

interpreted in such very different, and indeed wholly contradictory, fashions. For his career came at a critical turning-point of history; indeed it constituted the critical turning-point itself. That is why some writers interpret Caesar as the founder of a new era, while others prefer to see him as the terminator of an old one. That he completed the destruction of the old, collapsing Republican epoch cannot be denied. Lucan was right when he saw the battle of Pharsalus as the symbol of this demolition.

> Nor Fortune lingered, but decreed the doom
> Which swept the ruins of a world away.
> (Lucan, *Pharsalia*, VII, 504–5)

On the other hand to credit Caesar with the foundation of the new imperial age that followed is scarcely correct. Either because he did not live long enough to undertake more than a fraction of the vast work of reconstruction, or because careful constitutional patterns and façades did not appeal to him, he brought the Republican system to its inevitable end without finding anything new or acceptable to put in its place. Nevertheless, by a large number of reforming measures redolent of a new atmosphere of efficiency, and more particularly by the demonstration that one-man rule in Rome could work – if it was designed with more tactfulness than his own – it was he who prepared the way for the imperial regime that followed. And it was by learning from his achievements and mistakes alike that his grand-nephew Augustus became the first Roman emperor.

Further Reading

Ancient sources

The principal ancient authorities are Caesar's own informative but self-justificatory *Commentaries* (*Gallic War*, Books I–VII, and *Civil War*, I–III), together with Aulus Hirtius' eighth book of the *Gallic War*, and anonymous accounts of the Alexandrian, African and Spanish Wars; the voluminous writings of Cicero, and especially more than seven hundred of his letters *To Atticus* and *To Friends*, and some letters from his correspondents; the biographies of Suetonius (in Latin) and Plutarch (in Greek); Lucan's epic poem *The Civil War*, more widely known as the *Pharsalia*; Appian's *Civil Wars* and the *Histories* of Dio Cassius, both in Greek; and Sallust's *Catiline*. Coins, inscriptions, papyri, works of art, and remains of buildings are also extremely important, and it is perhaps through further study of the remarkable coinage of Caesar and his contemporaries that fresh gains in our knowledge will continue to be registered in the years immediately ahead.

Some modern biographies of Caesar

J.P.V.D.Balsdon, *Julius Caesar and Rome,* 1967, 1971.
M.Gelzer, *Caesar: Politician and Statesman,* 1968 (from the German of 1921, with revisions).
M.Grant, *Julius Caesar,* 1969, 1972.
H.Oppermann, *Caesar: Wegbereiter Europas,* 1958.
D.Rasmussen, *Caesar,* 1967.

Special studies of Caesar

F.E.Adcock, *Caesar as Man of Letters,* 1956.
G.Dobesch, *Caesars Apotheose zu Lebzeiten und sein Ringen um den Königstitel,* 1966.
J.F.C.Fuller, *Julius Caesar: Man, Soldier and Tyrant,* 1965.
M.Gelzer, *Cicero and Caesar,* 1968.
M.Grant, *Cleopatra,* 1972, 1974.
A.Momigliano, *Per un riesame della storia dell'idea di Cesarismo,* in: *Cesare nel bimillenario della morte,* 1956.
O.Seel, *Caesar-Studien,* 1967.
H.Strasburger, *Caesar im Urteil seiner Zeitgenossen,* 1953, 1968.
S.Weinstock, *Divus Julius,* 1971.

Background studies

E.Badian, *Roman Imperialism in the Late Republic,* 1967.
P.A.Brunt, *Italian Manpower 225 BC – AD 14,* 1971.
Cambridge Ancient History, Vol IX, 1932.
M.H.Crawford, *Roman Republican Coinage,* 1973.

J.Harmand, *L'armée et le soldat à Rome de 107 à 50 avant notre ère,* 1967.

P.Jal, *La guerre civile à Rome: étude littéraire et morale,* 1963

A.W.Lintott, *Violence in Republican Rome,* 1968.

H.H.Scullard, *From the Gracchi to Nero,* 1959, 1970.

R.Syme, *The Roman Revolution,* 1939, 1971.

C.Wirszubski, *Libertas as a Political Idea,* 1950.

List of Illustrations

*From J.F.C.Fuller, *Julius Caesar: Man, Soldier and Tyrant,* Eyre and Spottiswoode, 1965.

227

207 Coin of Augustus. *London, British Museum.*
208 The Vienna Cameo. *Vienna, Kunsthistorisches Museum.*
209 Coin of Galba. *London, British Museum.*
209 Coin of Trajan. *London, British Museum.*
211 Coin of Constantine the Great. *London, British Museum.*
214–5 Scene from *The Triumph of Caesar* by Andrea Mantegna. *Hampton Court, Royal Collections* (by courtesy of HM the Queen).
218–9 Tapestry with Julius Caesar on horseback. *Florence, Villa Reale della Petraia* (photograph ALINARI).

Maps drawn by Design Practitioners Limited.

Acknowledgments
The author owes acknowledgment to the following for quotations: Caesar, *The Civil War,* translated by Jane F. Mitchell, Penguin Classics 1967; Caesar, *The Conquest of Gaul,* tr. S.A.Handford, Penguin Classics 1951; Plutarch, *The Fall of the Roman Republic,* tr. Rex Warner, Penguin Classics 1958; *The Poems of Catullus,* tr. Peter Whigham, Penguin Classics 1966; *The Poems of Catullus,* tr. James Michie, Rupert Hart-Davis 1969; *Suetonius: The Twelve Caesars* (verses), tr. Robert Graves, Penguin Classics 1957.

Index